Kidwatching

Documenting Children's Literacy Development

Gretchen Owocki
Yetta Goodman

HEINEMANN
Portsmouth, NH

Heinemann
A division of Reed Elsevier Inc.
361 Hanover Street
Portsmouth, NH 03801–3912
www.heinemann.com

Offices and agents throughout the world

The author and publisher wish to thank those who have generously given permission to reprint borrowed material:

"Getting to Know Your Child" and "My Child as a Language Learner" are adapted from *Whole Language Catalog: Forms for Authentic Assessment* by Lois Bridges Bird, Ken Goodman, and Yetta Goodman. Copyright © 1994. Published by McGraw-Hill. Reprinted by permission of the authors.

"Child's Concepts of Reading" and "Child's Concepts of Written and Pictorial Representation" adapted from *Whole Language Catalog: Supplement on Authentic Assessment* by Lois Bridges Bird, Ken Goodman, and Yetta Goodman. Copyright © 1992. Published by McGraw-Hill. Reprinted by permission of the authors.

Library of Congress Cataloging-in-Publication Data
Owocki, Gretchen.
    Kidwatching : documenting children's literacy development / Gretchen Owocki, Yetta Goodman.
        p.   cm.
    ISBN 0-325-00461-7 (alk. paper)
    1. Language arts (Early childhood).   I. Goodman, Yetta M., 1931–.
II. Title.

LB1139.5.L35 O85 2002
372.6—dc21   2002004350

Editor: Lois Bridges
Production: Vicki Kasabian
Interior and cover photographs: Joel Brown
Cover design: Catherine Hawkes, Cat & Mouse
Author photo: Alan Flurkey
Typesetter: Publishers' Design and Production Services, Inc.
Manufacturing: Steve Bernier

Printed in the United States of America on acid-free paper
09 08 07 06   VP   8 9 10

To the thousands of children

and many hundreds of teachers

who taught us the power of kidwatching.

Contents

ACKNOWLEDGMENTS   vii

PREFACE   ix

Chapter 1   What Is Kidwatching?   1

Chapter 2   Sociocultural Knowledge and Experience   15

Chapter 3   Print Awareness   27

Chapter 4   Books and Book Handling   37

Chapter 5   Talk   48

Chapter 6   Oral Reading and Miscues   61

Chapter 7   Writing   77

Appendix   Reproducibles   95

BIBLIOGRAPHY   123

INDEX   129

Acknowledgments

We wish to thank the teachers and writers who contributed to the kid-watching and print awareness guides at the University of Arizona—Bess Altwerger, Ann (Marek) Anderson, Lois (Bird) Bridges, Jane Disinger, Nancy Earle, Kenneth Goodman, Wendy (Hood) Goodman, Don Howard, Debra Jacobson, Mary Kitagawa, Carol Woodley, John Woodley, Jackie Wortman, Robert Wortman—and all the other whole language teachers who continue to inform our thinking.

Preface

I am the teacher who is committed to discovering what each of my students knows, cares about, and can do.

I am the teacher who wants to understand each of my student's ways of constructing and expressing knowledge.

I am the teacher who helps my students connect what they are learning to what they already know.

I am the teacher who respects the language and culture my students learn at home, and who supports the expansion of this knowledge at school.

I am the teacher who knows that there are multiple paths to literacy, and who teaches along each child's path.

I am the teacher who is committed to social justice and to understanding literacy as a sociocultural practice.

I am the teacher who believes that each child can teach me about teaching, language, and learning.

I am the teacher who believes in the interconnectedness of language, learning, and life.

I am the teacher who supports children in writing *I can!* on their wings.

I am a kidwatcher.

Kidwatching: Documenting Children's Literacy Development is a guidebook for preschool, kindergarten, and primary teachers and paraprofessionals wishing to develop and refine their kidwatching (literacy evaluation) practices, and for anyone interested in developing new understandings about how children think and learn. The primary goals of kidwatching are to support and gain insight into children's learning by (1) intensely observing and documenting what they know and can do; (2) documenting their ways of constructing and expressing knowledge; and (3) planning curriculum and instruction that are tailored to individual strengths and needs. This book will help you learn to kidwatch and, specifically, to develop your knowledge about how children come to know literacy.

In Chapter 1, we answer the question "What is kidwatching?" and provide a description of the tools, techniques, and processes kidwatchers use as they observe and interact with children. Chapters 2 through 7 address particular areas to kidwatch: sociocultural knowledge and experience; print awareness; books and book handling; talk; oral reading and miscues; and writing. Each chapter provides a description of how kidwatching enhances teaching and learning; guidelines and suggestions for kidwatching; and practical tools and resources for documentation and analysis. Rather than a set of directions, you will find a set of potentials to choose from, shape, and adapt to meet your specific needs and interests. Kidwatching looks different from person to person; classroom to classroom; and year to year because each group of children is unique, each educator is unique, and teachers are continually developing and refining their practices.

Whether you are a paraprofessional, teacher, or teacher researcher, it is likely that your interest in kidwatching stems from a desire to enhance your teaching and improve student learning. Kidwatching helps you with this by guiding you through the following:

▶ learning about children in terms of their identities, experiences, interests, attitudes, family language and literacy practices, and familial and cultural backgrounds

▶ documenting what individual students know and can do

▶ using what you learn about individual children and general patterns of development to plan curriculum and instruction

▶ assessing how the class is doing in terms of meeting curricular goals (whether established at the individual, classroom, state, or national level); reflecting on whether the classroom instruction, materials, physical environment, and social environment provide a variety of ways to meet these goals, in keeping with what is known about child development

▶ involving students and families in the evaluation process

As you engage in kidwatching, you will find that you are *revaluing* children. To revalue is to notice and build on what learners can do, and to help them value and reflect on the knowledge they have (K. Goodman 1996b). *Value* is at the heart of words such as *evaluation* and *revalue*. Rather than viewing some children as "low" or "behind" or "lacking in skills," kidwatching teachers view all children as creative, capable learners—on their way to "achieving control over the conventions of language—always 'in process,' always moving forward . . . " (Flurkey 1997, 219). When observing through a kidwatching lens, beginning kidwatchers are always amazed by the intellectual curiosity and learning ingenuity of their students. They learn that while every child needs support in some areas, every child also has strengths.

Each chapter promotes revaluing by suggesting ways to partner with children to document and reflect on their knowledge. The documentation is used to highlight and discuss with children their strengths, interests, and approaches to learning; help them identify their productive (and nonproductive) reading, writing, and learning strategies; and determine next steps in teaching and learning. Such processes provide important information for parents, future teachers, and permanent school records. Thus, in kidwatchers' classrooms, children are empowered to evaluate and revalue themselves.

The Origins of Kidwatching

Kidwatching has been around for as long as the teaching profession, but the 1930s gave rise to a particularly innovative child-study movement that led to its eventual expansion and refinement. Many educators by the 1930s had begun to carefully observe children, reflecting extensively on their oral and written language use. Although these educators did not refer to themselves as kidwatchers, they were kidwatching—using children's demonstrated strengths and needs to inform curriculum and instruction.

Yetta's work from the 1970s and '80s served to popularize the concept of kidwatching by giving it definition and helping teachers and researchers learn to use it to structure and enhance their work. As her work with kidwatching and kidwatchers has evolved over the past thirty years, so too has the concept (see Y. Goodman 1996a, 1996b; Martens 1997; O'Keefe 1996; Owocki 1999; Whitmore and Goodman 1995).

Before We Begin: A Thought About Standardized Testing

Many parents, educators, and administrators are currently dismayed by the heightened national emphasis on standardized testing. First, pressure to do well on standardized tests often changes how and what we teach. Because standardized tests focus on low-level skills, simple facts, and demonstrations of skills in isolation, many teachers feel pressured to focus their instruction in these areas. Second, although "good" test results are valued by many, standardized tests do not serve instructional purposes. They do not help teachers plan meaningful learning experiences because they cannot reveal the competencies that children demonstrate in familiar, everyday home and school settings. Many young children are easily distracted during testing situations, have anxiety about the process, do not easily follow verbally mediated test directions, and have no experience with testlike activities (Hills 1999; Meisels 1995; Salinger 1998). Third, many students' language and cultural experiences differ vastly from those specific kinds that would help them do well on tests. Any time a state or country full of children is held up to a single model of success, we risk losing our focus on supporting all children. Finally, tests reveal little about children's approaches to learning and ways of constructing knowledge.

Kidwatching offers a solution. It provides a framework for engaging in systematic, yet very personalized, data collection in all areas of literacy. High-quality kidwatching gives you the information you need to teach effectively, to work with child study teams, and to share detailed, concrete information with families and administrators. Students benefit from your in-depth understandings of their knowledge and ways of knowing, and parents prefer the rich assessment information over scores from multiple-choice tests (Neill 2000).

Kidwatching can also be used to strengthen school reform. The classroom-based assessments provide more helpful profiles of individual students than standardized tests, and can be used to construct schoolwide systems of assessment that actually support student learning (Neill 2000). Groups of teachers, administrators, and family members working together can use kidwatching techniques, along with knowledge about their particular students, contexts, and communities, to develop a common set of principles and evaluation practices that are in tune with local needs and interests. "Students come from many cultures and languages. Instruction and assessment should connect to the local and the culturally particular and not presume uniformity of experience, culture, language, and ways of knowing" (Neill 2000, 138). Focusing on practices that place children in the safe nest of hands formed by teachers and families helps assessment maintain its ideal function—to support student learning.

Reproducibles, found full-size in the appendix, are shown in smaller versions in the text.

What Is Kidwatching?

It's Friday morning in Jacquie Whitmore's first- and second-grade classroom. The children are engaged in activities of choice, and Jacquie is kidwatching. Jacquie has agreed on this morning to do a think-aloud—to share what goes on in her kidwatching mind as she observes her students daily at work and play. As she stands looking over the class, she notices that two separate groups of children have gathered to make posters for Secretary Appreciation Day. Jacquie checks in with each group, noting that the children have written messages on the posters and signed their names. Raymond is working alone on a poster but has not written a message. When Jacquie encourages him to "write something so that the secretary will know who made the poster," Raymond responds, "I can't remember how to spell *from*."

Jacquie refers him to the class word wall, where he correctly identifies the word before copying it onto his poster.

Jacquie thinks aloud about her kidwatching: *I like Friday mornings. I purposefully use this choice time to connect with kids and understand who they are as learners. This is a time for them to pursue their own questions and develop their own strategies. It's a time for me to capture teachable moments.*

Two children are snuggled on the couch reading an alphabet book. Jacquie pauses briefly to observe. Jacquie: *I take more written notes when I conference individually with students. Right now, I'm making mental notes. It's different from what another teacher might do in that some teachers approach a class with a focus on a prescribed curriculum—they "know" what first graders need and teach it to a sea of students.*

I'm taking this time to learn about my kids and their differences, to see what they can do, and also to determine how I can best support their needs. Jacquie illustrates that kidwatching is as much a state of mind as a collection of techniques for gathering and reflecting on data. It is about getting to know students through observing them intelligently—and helping them work through the concepts and language issues they are raising in their own minds.

Another part of what Jacquie observes through kidwatching is the ways in which her students interact socially, and, in general, negotiate their days. For example, when Dawn, arms folded across her chest, walks in late with a glaring frown on her face, Jacquie is watching. When Dawn roughly attempts to join a group of poster makers, who try to stop her, Jacquie is watching. What makes the kidwatcher in Jacquie stand out is her positive focus on what Dawn can do and her desire to understand her students: *Dawn always comes in like that, but did you see her look at the schedule? She's reading the morning schedule and trying to fit in.* When Jacquie is eventually consulted to help resolve the situation with Dawn, she first asks the children what is happening and how they have tried to solve their problem. As a kidwatcher, Jacquie is always focused on understanding the ways in which her students are problem solving and using language so that she can help them expand their repertoires of possibilities.

Jacquie: *Lately, a lot of kids seem to be coming to me for help with things they could probably handle themselves . . . so I've been wondering if I'm encouraging that too much.* Kidwatching teachers reflect on their own practices. Jacquie knows that fertile conditions for learning must be in place if children are to fully demonstrate their knowledge. The community must be caring, the environment must be rich, and the children must feel safe to take the kinds of risks that enable them to show their understandings, explore their questions, and work with challenging concepts and material. As Jacquie kidwatches, she regularly thinks about

what she can do to fortify the learning environment. Kidwatching helps her refine her philosophy and her teaching.

When most of Jacquie's students are settled, she gathers some materials for listening to and documenting children's oral readings and retellings. She invites Chad and then Dawn to read for her, recording their miscues and filling in a form she has prepared for retellings. Jacquie: *It doesn't take long to squeeze in individualized sessions like this. Documenting miscues helps me understand how to help with reading. Dawn is predicting as she reads, but she doesn't recognize many sight words and needs more strategies for analyzing unknown words. I can use this information to help Dawn develop these strategies by placing her in a temporary group with children who have similar needs.*

The children line up at the door, ready to go to their music class. Taffy, bedecked in dark sunglasses, lingers behind, looking at an arrangement of seed packets. She and Jacquie talk for a few minutes about their plans for gardens in the spring. Taffy advises Jacquie on the kinds of corn that will grow in Alaska and asks if she can take home a packet of corn seeds for her grandmother. Jacquie: *I can definitely use the kind of information that Taffy just shared. I'll let her take home the seeds, and maybe we'll see about a journal for recording plant growth. I can also find her some books about seeds.*

Observing Jacquie, one sees that kidwatching does not interrupt or get in the way of children's learning. At the same time as students are involved in the learning plans for the day, Jacquie is involved in teaching, evaluation, and curriculum development. In her classroom, this means reaching carefully into children's worlds to help them build from the known, expand to the unknown, and expand their ways of constructing and expressing knowledge. For a kidwatcher, time spent observing, gathering data, and interacting with children is time well spent.

Jacquie is engaged on this Friday morning in the basic acts of *kidwatching*. She is (1) taking note of what her students know and can do; (2) attempting to understand their ways of constructing and expressing knowledge; and (3) using what she learns to shape her curriculum and instruction. Her observations and the wealth of data she collects enable her to respond to children in helpful, effective ways. The more Jacquie learns about her students through kidwatching, the better able she is to individualize and fine-tune her instruction. In the following sections, we describe the processes that make kidwatching work to its fullest potential:

▶ building an insider view of the community

▶ understanding how language and literacy develop

▶ organizing a rich environment for learning

▶ interacting with children

▶ observing and documenting children's knowledge

▶ analyzing data

▶ fostering children's self-evaluation

▶ engaging in self-evaluation of teaching

▶ using evaluation to inform instruction and build curriculum

Building an Insider View

Successful kidwatchers like Jacquie intentionally build an insider view of their students and the culture of their classrooms. In ethnographic research the *emic*, or insider's view, is essential to understanding a cultural community and the individuals within that community. Ethnographers value careful observation of phenomena by knowledgeable observers who spend time watching, interacting, taking notes, and making professionally informed interpretations (Y. Goodman 1996a). Kidwatchers add one important component to this list: they make professionally

informed teaching decisions based on the data they collect.

The aim of kidwatching is not only to "become more and more reflectively aware of the frames of interpretation [of your students but also to become more aware of your] own culturally learned frames of interpretation" (Erickson 1986, 140). It is not enough to develop insight into children's ways of thinking about and understanding the world; you must also develop insight into your own. What are your beliefs about literacy? Where do they come from? How do these beliefs influence your interpretation of classroom events and your instructional decisions? Dewey argues that "thinking in its best sense is that which considers the basis and consequences of beliefs" ([1910] 1997, 5). We believe that the same holds true of teaching. Effective teachers consciously consider what they believe about language, learning, children, and their worlds. They also consider where their beliefs come from, and how their beliefs influence the interpretations and decisions they make in the classroom. We have included questions in some of the subsequent chapters that will guide you to reflect on your personal beliefs and the ways in which they influence your teaching.

Understanding How Language and Literacy Develop

A second component of successful kidwatching is to understand how language and literacy develop. Most kidwatchers we know are informed by a *developmental, sociocultural* perspective on language and learning. Such a perspective is steeped in the notion that children *construct* knowledge within *unique social worlds*.

Knowledge Construction
Knowledge construction happens as children develop and test a never-ending series of hypotheses, or ideas, about the ways in which language works. For example, young writers often hypothesize that their squiggle marks or

random strings of letters spell words. "What does this say?" they ask, or "Look! I wrote *Mama*." Similarly, young readers may hypothesize that the logo on a soup can says "soup" (instead of *Campbell's*) or that the brand name on a refrigerator says "frigerator" (instead of *Amana*). Talkers test hypotheses, too. When four-year-old Cynthia says, "There's some beautiful womans in here," or six-year-old Kiara says, "My mom packed-ed me some pudding," it is easy to see that these children are bringing their knowledge together and trying to organize it into something meaningful. Research in all areas of language—speaking, listening, reading, and writing—suggests that children's hypotheses or "errors" or "miscues" are not random and in most cases can be explained by understanding how people learn. What an adult assumes to be erroneous often reflects development in the child. Children's expressions of language, or inventions, reflect their current schemas, or working models for how language works.

"When objects, events, and other people challenge the working model, the child adjusts it to account for the new information" (Bredekamp and Copple 1997, 13). From a developmental, sociocultural perspective, learning is a process of *becoming* and children become literate as internal and social forces work together to shape their understandings. When internal and social forces meet (when children meaningfully connect their ways of thinking with objects, events, and people in the environment), a sense of cognitive *tension* (Goodman and Goodman 1990) or *disequilibrium* (Ferreiro and Teberosky 1982; Piaget 1952) is often the result. That is because social experiences (which present conventional literacy information) don't always completely fit within children's working models (which often reflect their own inventions). When children experience such tension, they actively seek to reinstate a sense of equilibrium. For example, seven-year-old Ivy was playing school one day when she noticed the word *they* in print. "What does this say," she asked, "because I know T-H-A-Y spells *they*?" Ivy's experience with convention did not fit into her working model; therefore, she sought the information she needed to expand her model, or to assimilate the information.

According to Piaget, sometimes the tension is not so easy, and children must significantly reorganize the schema, or accommodate, to make the new information fit. For example, Archie, a first grader rehearsing a readers theater script, was repeatedly reading "I could it," instead of the words he had copied on his paper: *I knew it*. Finally, he pointed to the "tricky" word and asked, "What *is* this?" Upon discovering that the word was *knew*, he looked as if in disbelief, and countered, "But it starts with a K!" Based on his experiences and history with print, Archie had developed a hypothesis about the sound that K could represent. Because his understanding was not yet fully developed, it was challenged and mediated—in this case, by both print *and* his social experience. When children's current working models (their current hypotheses) are challenged or mediated in a comprehensible way (either socially or by print itself), they rethink or reorganize them and move toward new understandings. In this way, social experiences become part of children's literacy histories.

Personal and Sociocultural Influences

The vast differences both in individual children and in the objects, events, and people in their worlds make knowledge construction a different experience for every child. Some children are notoriously interested in exploring written language. Any chance they get, they have their hands on pencils, paper, books, magazines, maps, catalogs, computers—or whatever literacy materials they have in their environments. These children want to know what everybody's writing, what every sign says, what everybody's reading, and who wrote it. Other children don't pay much attention to print; either they aren't interested, they haven't yet discovered print's functions, or they're busy doing other things such as playing with toy cars, building with blocks, riding bicycles, or watching television.

Children's unique interests, favored activities, print features they attend to, ways of knowing, and dispositions influence how and to what extent they participate in early literacy events, and, in turn, the knowledge they construct.

Families contribute another layer of influence to children's literacy. Some families actively involve their children in reading the mail, listening to and telling stories, helping with the shopping, or participating in work-related activities. They may read newspapers together, write cards together, go to the bank together, or share materials from religious and cultural events. In some homes, children participate in such events in Spanish, Chinese, Hmong, or Russian, often in addition to English. In some homes, children are exposed to print in more peripheral ways. These children undoubtedly see print being used (often in more than one language), but for a variety of possible reasons, it remains primarily in the hands of others. Because different families and different cultural groups stress different kinds of activity, knowledge, uses of language, values, work, social interactions, and social organization, children develop different knowledge, and they develop knowledge differently. Individual, familial, social, and cultural forces make each child's literacy history unique.

Figure 1–1 shows that the changes that children make as they become literate extend in many directions. Rather than building one language concept at a time, children simultaneously build knowledge about myriad aspects of language, including its functions, formats, genres, meanings, sounds, grammars, visual features, and spellings (represented by solid lines). When they experience moments of tension or disequilibrium, or place their focus on new literacy concepts, things may appear to fall apart (represented by zigzag lines). Overall, the knowledge children develop, and the way they develop that knowledge, is shaped by their sociocultural experiences (represented by dotted lines). Because children have an influence on the nature of many sociocultural experiences, some

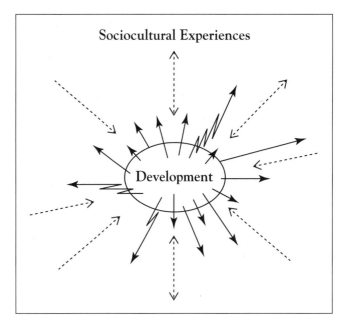

FIGURE 1–1   The Nature of Development

of the dotted lines have arrows going in two directions.

All children have literacy knowledge. In a general sense, the richer and more varied the settings and interactions, the richer the child's language and concepts will be. In a kidwatching classroom, *rich* is not absently interpreted from a school-based cultural view; nor is it narrowly defined. A sociocultural pedagogy expects "rich" to be different for every child (Oakes and Lipton 1999). Therefore, a rich experience is one that is socially and culturally meaningful *to the children having the experience*. A rich experience could range from planting strawberries to making a board game; from listening to an old aunt tell stories to taking a silent walk down a city street; from making a family recipe to writing in Spanish to relatives living in Mexico. Because rich is a construct that is socially and culturally determined, it is important to leave room for its interpretation in your classroom. Given the opportunity, your students and their families will teach you what rich means to them, and you can use that information to create a classroom that welcomes diversity. In the following sections, as we discuss organizing rich environments for observation and interaction, it is important to consider what *rich* means to you as well as to your particular students.

Organizing a Rich Environment for Learning

In order to gain useful information from kidwatching, it is necessary to organize a rich environment for learning. Evaluation provides the most significant information when it occurs simultaneously with learning experiences—as children read, write, listen, speak, perform, present, and play. In the Reggio Emilia approach to education—an approach originating in northern Italy, grounded in respect for children, their families, their communities, and their cultures—documentation is a regular part of classroom practice. Educators involved with this approach find that documentation enhances learning by showing value for children's thinking, by fostering planning between teachers and children, and by making children's learning visible. These contributions to learning became possible "because children are engaged in absorbing, complex, interesting projects worthy of documentation" (Katz and Chard 1996, 4). Children are most apt to show us what they know and can do as they engage in meaningful learning experiences. Because students show different capabilities in different contexts, kidwatchers observe them as they use language in a variety of settings, on a variety of topics, and through interaction with a variety of people.

Interacting with Children

Your interactions with children as they engage in learning experiences play an important part in kidwatching—and an important part in their growth. Vygotsky describes a child's *zone of proximal development* as a cognitive state in which he or she can do with an adult or more capable peer what he or she cannot do alone. Tasks or activities within a child's zone are challenging to the child, but achievable with support; they are neither too familiar nor too

far beyond the child's current understandings. Kidwatchers intentionally seek out this zone, recognizing that "what a child can do with assistance today, she will be able to do by herself tomorrow" (Vygotsky 1978, 87). Evaluating what a child can do with guidance helps you plan immediate or future experiences that capitalize on the child's current intellectual functioning.

To keep interactions within children's zones, teachers aim at supporting new ways of thinking while ensuring that the children's curiosity for the experience remains intact. This requires an artful blend of following and leading at the same time; a skillful combination of knowing when to participate and question, and when to watch and follow. The idea is to help children see things in new ways based on the competencies they demonstrate. To do so, kidwatchers are always asking appropriate questions, posing problems relevant to children's thinking, helping children pose, develop, and refine their own questions and problems, and challenging them to explore beyond what they are thinking at the moment. In other words, the adult thinks through, or "negotiates," concepts with the child, providing ideas and support as, if, and when they are needed (Bruner 1983). Such transactions gently invite children to consider conflicting, different, or more complex information, and often lead to moments of disequilibrium. As we saw earlier, such moments lead children to reorganize and rethink their concepts and ideas.

Interacting during kidwatching also involves *interpretive probing* (Mickleson 1990)— asking questions in order to discover what children know and why they think the way they do. For example, asking "What makes you think so?" or "Why did you choose to do it this way?" gives a teacher particular insights into a child's thinking and reasoning processes, and often entices the child into further inquiry, or disequilibrium. Such questions help children, too, to critically examine their own knowledge base and to reflect on their own learning.

Interpretive probing is also useful in small- or whole-group settings because it helps children extend their thinking by listening to and talking with others. You can prompt interpretive conversations by asking questions such as What did you notice the snails doing today? What did you wonder about? Why do you think Yasir's puppy was panting? What makes you think so? Children's responses to such questions are invaluable in helping you learn about their knowledge and plan future instructional and curricular experiences within their zones of proximal development.

More formal interactional time is also planned. Regularly planned conferences or instructional sessions (individual or small group) provide opportunities for addressing the needs of individuals and getting specific information about their reading, writing, and thinking. These sessions are planned for very specific purposes. For example, you could tape-record a child reading a passage and then analyze together the miscues that were made. You could gather a group to edit their own or a piece of class writing. Or, you could present a group of children with a cloze passage (selected words missing), supporting and observing their conversation as they decide what the missing words might be. Such activities give you insight into what students know about language as well as the content of the material, and they help students become more consciously aware of their own thinking processes.

Observing and Documenting Children's Knowledge

Observation and documentation are about "getting to know each child in as many different contexts as possible—to know each child as a person unique in all the world" (O'Keefe 1996). The first step in observation is having up-to-date knowledge about language—about general patterns of development as well as the sociocultural nature of language learning. General patterns serve as indicators of growth and guide teachers in

determining where to go next in their planning and instruction. Researchers have documented general developmental patterns in areas such as print awareness, book handling, reading, writing, and spelling. In subsequent chapters, some of the checklists we include reflect general developmental patterns. However, kidwatching teachers don't let general patterns get in the way of discovering the uniqueness of each child. They know that each child's developmental sequence is different. Children often surprise us with their fresh and inventive views of the world.

It is also important in observation to be aware of the role of error in language learning. Because errors, inventions, and miscues are expressions of language and concepts as they currently exist in the child's schema, they are thoughtfully documented and studied by kidwatchers. As children develop conceptually and linguistically, kidwatchers watch for errors (inventions, miscues) to shift from representing unsophisticated conclusions to showing greater sophistication (Dewey [1910] 1997; Ferreiro and Teberosky 1982).

As a kidwatcher, it is important to help children and families understand that errors are really not mistakes. Developmentally, errors (we prefer the terms *inventions* and *miscues*) are to be expected. Dewey argues that insisting upon avoidance of error tends to interrupt children's discourse and thought, and may cause hesitancy in their willingness to express themselves through language. "Children who begin with something to say and with intellectual eagerness to say it are sometimes made so conscious of minor errors in substance and form that the energy that should go into constructive thinking is diverted into anxiety not to make mistakes, and even, in extreme cases, into passive quiescence as the best method of minimizing error" (Dewey [1910] 1997, 186). Allowing errors does not equate with negligent teaching. In fact, teachers who "do not allow errors to occur . . . do not allow children to think" (Ferreiro and Teberosky 1982, 218). Children do not refine their hypotheses because we tell them they are wrong or tell them the right way. They refine hypotheses as they actively explore them, try them out in all kinds of social situations, and receive instruction within their zones of proximal development. Kidwatchers track progress over time by documenting children's knowledge, including that which is revealed through their unconventional uses of language. And, instead of using the terms *mistake* or *wrong*, they use *miscue* and *invention* to value children's constructions.

The central task of observation is to document what children know, as well as their ways of constructing and expressing knowledge. Observation and documentation happen when you step aside from your oral interactions with children to observe from the sidelines or when you interact with your whole class, meet with a small group, confer with a single student, or participate in a quick over-the-shoulder conference. Sometimes you capture observations through anecdotal notes, while other times you collect artifacts such as oral reading samples, taped recordings of children's reading, retellings, responses to literature, writing samples, answers to interview questions, and children's self-reflections on their learning. To organize yourself to observe each child, it is helpful to establish a routine. Some teachers, along with regular informal observations, plan to intensively observe every student at least once every two weeks. They make a schedule that involves observing two to three children per day. Other teachers do such recordings once a month or twice a semester.

Anecdotal Records

The general procedure for recording observations is to rotate around the room at different times of the day or week, taking anecdotal notes and collecting artifacts from each student working in different content areas, different settings, and different kinds of activities. For example, you might record children's choices during play, the strategies they use as they read and write, or the oral language they use as they participate in literacy events. The key is to focus on the kinds of information that will inform your instructional decision making. You may find it helpful to keep a few notebooks or pads of sticky notes in strategic places around the classroom so that you do not "lose" important critical moments. Or, prepare a note-taking form with the name of each child on it (see Figure 1–2) and keep a few of those around the classroom.

Another option is to prepare one form per child (see Figure 1–3). A quick note on such a form can stand by itself or be expanded at a more convenient time. Many teachers take ten minutes at the end of the day to catch up on their note taking and reflect on the events of the day. This happens after the children go home, or just before they leave, as they are writing or drawing to reflect on their learning (Short, Harste, and Burke 1996).

Yet another option is to record notes of a more specific, planned nature. For example, you may decide to focus in depth on one child's reading strategies, writing strategies, talk, interests, or attitudes—or all of these (see Figure 1–4). Such notes, particularly useful for students who need extra support from you, are kept in the student's personal work folder so that they can be reflected on and referred to again and again.

Field Notes

Field notes are useful when you are observing for extended periods of time (three to ten minutes). They include in-depth descriptions of children's solitary activity and social interactions, often in the form of scripts. Field notes should be planned strategically, at times when you are likely to see the kinds of activity that are most informative for your literacy instruction. An example from Christian Bush's first-grade classroom is shown in Figure 1–5. In the example, Archie and Robert are in the midst of writing a text for a wordless picture book; Christian observes and documents for approximately ten minutes.

Teachers gain many insights into children's knowledge and thinking as they ana-

Angelica 3/1 Reads Brown Bear aloud—points to words *Arrange for A. to read aloud to class	Aurora	Diego	Edilberto 3/3 Tells Josh how to spell love (LVOE) 3/8 Lists things he likes: PL (pool), MOM, POKEMON
Hannah	Ivy	Jacob	Joshua
Jordan	Lauren	Lavonya 3/1 Observing Angelica. Points out to me the rhymes in Brown Bear	Madison
-Matthew 3/1 Guinness Record book—again. * I need to read sections aloud to whole class.	Marlie	Megan	Michael
Noah	Pao 3/8 Using English in Science Center: "float" "sink" "try this"	Piper Kay 3/3 Drawing/talking about Pokemon. 3/8 Pokemon. Labels characters when suggested.	Preston
Ronnie	Taylor	Ty'Ree	William

FIGURE 1–2   Sample Note-Taking Form for Whole-Class Observations

lyze field notes. For example, Christian's field notes reveal that Archie:

► contributes ideas directly related to the pictures

► makes connections across pages

► understands importance of rereading for meaning

► brings in personal experiences not directly referenced in pictures

► attends to punctuation

Name: **Piper Kay**	
Literacy Event and Date:	**Instructional Implications:**
4/22 medical chart notes on height	show different ways ht. measures are written
4/29 pretends a blank piece of paper is a menu	suggest menu-making/ bring in menus for play
5/6 writing prices for items on menu	use menus to show how to note monetary values

FIGURE 1–3   Note-Taking Form for Single-Child Observations

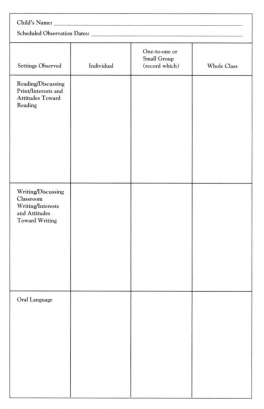

Reproducible, see p. 96

FIGURE 1–4   Detailed Observation Form

- ▶ demonstrates concept of word
- ▶ breaks words into parts for spelling
- ▶ attends to legibility

Checklists

Checklists provide a quick way to record accomplishments, understandings, processes, or strategies. Depending on your purpose, they are designed to record one child's information, or information from the whole class. Chapters 2 through 7 provide a variety of checklists that you can use as starting points as you think through what is appropriate to evaluate in your own classroom. Ultimately, designing your own checklists is important because it compels you to consciously consider what *you* value and to establish criteria for analyzing *your* children's processes and products. Checklists are most useful during the first few months of the year as you are getting to know children and their competencies. As you know your students better, less formal observations are more easily made because you are more apt to spontaneously recognize information that will add to the profile of the student's knowledge and development. Checklists are most useful when you adapt them over the school year to match your children's development.

In using checklists, keep in mind that teachers typically do not look for elements of development that are simply "there" or "not there," but rather seek "to understand the children's personal language in order to help them become effective language users" (Mickleson 1990, 18). Thus, many teachers leave spaces on their checklists for filling in additional information. This way, the list provides a beginning organizational scheme for notes, but does not limit the information that may be recorded. Teachers tell us that they adapt their checklists often in response to what they learn through the kidwatching process.

Checklists also serve as a tool for analyzing data. For example, if you design a checklist that delineates writing strategies, you could use it as you examine your anecdotal notes

Wordless Picture Books/ February 10

Robert doing all writing.

Archie: Some food you have to peel. Some you got to peel . . . Some . . . got to be peeled. What
          do you have writed so far?
Robert: Some you peel.
Archie: Erase peel. Got. Gahhh.

Archie asks Robert to reread after every 2 words or so. Robert's spelling is pretty good, but
Archie's having difficulty reading it.

Archie: Let's do . . . uh, took—check their money, Robert. Check their money. Check . . . their . . .
money.
Robert: Where should I put it? [rereads] They are buying some food. Some are already buyed.
          There are some foods you got to peel. Some people check their lists. [writing and
          talking]
Archie: Some people hate fruit. Not don't like; hate fruit—I mean vegetables.

Robert writes "Some people hate vegetables."

Archie: Robert, that don't look like an O. [he erases and corrects] There are food on the
          counter—c-oun-t-er [says as to sound it out for Robert] Okay, Robert are you done?
Robert: Yeah.
Archie: Okay, put a period. The man buyed the food and then the children eat it. No, I mean
          cooks the food. She already buyed it.
Me: Make sure you practice reading this because you'll be recording it today.
Archie: What if I can't read it?
Me: You said most of the ideas . . .
Archie: Okay [hesitantly].

FIGURE 1–5   Christian's Field Notes

and writing samples. The checklist helps you identify the range of strategies that each child is currently using and plan specific kinds of instruction that are warranted. Note that many of Archie's listed strengths in the previous section reflect items typically included on a reading strategy checklist. Checklists that reflect developmental continua are also useful for showing changes in growth and development.

Whichever ways you choose to record, it is important to remember that the information you collect must be useful to you: it must be worth evaluating and must be revealing of children's knowledge and growth.

If any recording device you are using is not working, be sure to experiment with new techniques.

Analyzing Data

Analysis of reading, writing, and oral language happens during all parts of kidwatching—as you observe, interact, and reflect with children on their learning. The notes and artifacts you collect are invaluable tools that warrant careful attention because they provide you with deep insights into what children know and can do, as well as into their ways of constructing and expressing knowledge. These are essential insights for helping children build their language competencies.

To prepare materials for analysis, teachers typically organize them into some sort of folder. Sturdy folders with pockets and three prongs, or folders with a closing clasp or band, work well because they hold all sorts of materials and can be stored all together in a box. Consider including a date stamp near the box so that children can easily record the date before filing their material. Some possibilities for organization follow:

1. Place materials into general categories. Depending on your students, consider the following: (a) information on identity as a reader and writer; (b) book handling information; (c) oral reading and retelling audiotapes and notes; (d) writing samples; (e) projects; (f) information collected during play. Document knowledge and growth in each area.

2. Organize materials into three very general sections (reading; writing; oral language) with subcategories for each section. Document knowledge and growth in each area:

   A. reading
      1. reading samples
      2. print awareness inventory
      3. checklists and profile forms
      4. list of child's preferred genres and topics for reading
      5. list of books and other materials that have been read
      6. retellings, sketches, illustrations, and drawings used to share readings
      7. reading interviews and interest inventories
      8. self-evaluations
      9. anecdotal records and informal notes
   B. writing
      1. writing samples
      2. spelling evaluations
      3. list of child's preferred genres and topics for writing
      4. list of pieces written, including genres and topics
      5. self-evaluations
      6. checklists and profile forms
      7. anecdotal records and informal notes
   C. oral language
      1. retellings
      2. anecdotal records and informal notes
      3. notes and transcripts from literature discussions
      4. transcripts from discussions about a project
      5. oral presentations
      6. reporting in class about current events, readings, or topics of interest

Consider whether the materials you collect should be placed in a cumulative folder, in a work folder (some teachers call it a *portfolio*), or both. Work folders typically contain self- or jointly selected pieces of work from the child, audiotapes, the child's self-evaluations, and goals for future learning. These are the kinds of items that are regularly referred back to by teacher and child. Cumulative folders are kept by the teacher and used to document a child's full literacy learning history. Cumulative folders contain information that is used to report knowledge and growth over the years, and to share with children, families, other teachers, and administrators when appropriate. These are passed on with the child to the next grades.

Using Questions as a Basis for Analysis

Using a set of questions helps to focus your analysis. We use three general questions as we examine data: (1) What does the child know about language? (2) What evidence is there that language development is taking place? and (3) When a child produces something unexpected or unconventional, what does it tell about the child's knowledge of language? This information is used to plan curriculum and instruction. Following are some examples of more specific questions to consider:

▶ In which settings does the child use more or less oral language?

▶ In which settings does the child appear to be comfortable?

▶ In which contexts does the child work alone; seem to prefer to work with others?

▶ Is the child attentive during discussions when other children or the teacher is speaking?

▶ With which classmates does a less talkative child communicate the most?

▶ Which activities does the child initiate?

▶ In what ways does the child adapt and adjust language to new situations and settings?

▶ When is the child successful in getting things done?

▶ When does the child seem confused?

▶ In what settings does the child need further support?

Expect your questions to change as children change and develop, and as your knowledge of the class, your children, and child development changes and develops.

Fostering Children's Self-Evaluation

The most important type of evaluation is self-evaluation because it helps children become critically aware of their own thinking and learning processes. Even very young children are able to recognize their strengths, think about what they need to do and learn in order to accomplish their language goals, and consciously work toward improving in areas of need. When you share your collected information with your students, and invite them to collect and share information of their own, you support their self-evaluation. Individual, small-group, or whole-class confer-

ences can be used to help children understand the purposes of self-evaluation, to discuss how you document children's knowledge and growth, and to encourage children to self-evaluate by asking themselves the following questions:

▶ What do I know? What am I learning?

▶ What am I using reading and writing for? How else would I like to be able to use it? How can I learn to do that?

▶ What am I doing well? What could I improve?

▶ How are things going in particular areas (such as literature circles or writing workshop)? What can I do to make them go better next time?

▶ What goals do I hope to achieve?

Record younger children's responses for them, and help older children record their own. Self-evaluation helps students recognize the significance of their own learning and extends and refines the meaning of their learning experiences.

Kidwatchers and family members get together for evaluation conferences on a regular basis. Conferences enable you and your students to provide parents with a detailed account of children's capabilities and growth. In fact, the rich set of data enables parents to do their own evaluating. "Reporting progress to parents . . . is most successful when it helps [them] to evaluate growth themselves" (K. Goodman 1991, 252). Family members are encouraged to participate in other kidwatching processes as well. Many teachers invite parents to introduce their child early in the school year through face-to-face conferences or a personal letter. They invite them to take anecdotal notes (at home or school), collect children's writing samples, list what they read and write at home—and add all of this information to the child's work folder. Parents also fill out questionnaires, or dialogue in journals between home and school, to provide the teacher with extra insights and information.

Planning and reflecting with children and families help you get to know their experiences, interests, preferences, and goals, and to develop a shared sense of not only what is expected of children but also what is possible for them.

Engaging in Self-Evaluation of Teaching

Carefully observing children's progress helps you to thoughtfully evaluate your own progress as a teacher. As you are reflecting on children's activity, it is natural to reflect on the contributions you are making to their learning. The kinds of questions kidwatching teachers ask about themselves include the following:

▶ How do my interactions facilitate children's learning?

▶ What is working well and not working well?

▶ Am I providing materials, conditions, and experiences that allow my students to show what they know? What might prevent them from showing what they know?

▶ How might my beliefs about language and literacy influence the opportunities I provide?

▶ Am I allowing for exploration of multiple literacies?

Examining your own evaluation practices helps you reach new ground as an evaluator and makes evaluation a positive teaching-learning experience.

Using Evaluation to Inform Instruction

The purpose of kidwatching is to help children build their capabilities to use language to communicate and learn. Teachers achieve this by inquiring into who children are, what they know, what they can do, and how they learn. Because some knowledge is evident in children's daily language and actions, kidwatchers are always observing with a watchful, reflective eye. Because other knowledge lies beneath the surface, kidwatchers transact with children and their families to unearth what else is there. Teachers make these efforts in order to support children as they build upon their existing literacy knowledge and practices—or, in other words, in order "to keep alive the sacred spark of wonder and to fan the flame that already glows" (Dewey [1910] 1997, 33–34). Teaching with a kidwatching eye offers a dignity to children by affirming the legitimacy of their own experiences, and of using them to learn. And of course, in a classroom where children are so esteemed, there is dignity in teaching.

Sociocultural Knowledge and Experience

The children in Christian Bush's first-grade classroom are playing. Today, they are doctors, nurses, patients, weather reporters, meteorologists, teachers, and principals. As the children play, Christian documents their knowledge by taking field notes and collecting writing samples:

Notes from Weather Center: The children are drawing the states on the overhead projector and drawing symbols [suns, clouds] to represent the weather. Jacob holds the microphone and is very animated giving the weather report. "It is sunny in New York, very sunny! I mean hot! [Points to Texas.] Oooh . . . Texas has a little tornado problem—and a little icy."

Writing sample from Weather Center: in ohio tar was a tornedo! it nict the best hous over [In Ohio there was a tornado. It knocked the best house over.]

Writing sample from Doctor's Office: it moustleey herts in the acoll her hole lage is sweld time 3.00 at the parck in a three she has a brokin bowne. [It mostly hurts in the ankle. Her whole leg is swelled. Time 3:00. At the park in a tree. She has a broken bone.]

Kidwatchers learn much about children's sociocultural knowledge by observing them as they work and play. They learn about the places they've been, the people they've encountered, their oral and written language histories, and their resources for getting things accomplished. Delving into these sociocultural aspects of children's worlds is important because it reveals much about their literacies and provides ideas for supporting their further development. In this chapter we explore the central role that sociocultural experiences play in children's literacy development, and the techniques that kidwatchers use to learn about and capitalize on children's sociocultural knowledge and experiences.

Understanding Language as a Sociocultural Practice

Sociolinguistic theory and research indicate that language develops as a sociocultural practice. Children develop the capability to *use*, *talk about*, and *learn through* language (both oral and written) as they use it within the social and cultural contexts of their lives. Christian's classroom data helps illustrate this point. Observing her students at play reveals that these children have been out there in the world—building knowledge about people, places, objects, and events and, at the same time, about the language and literacy practices that are associated with these things. As they have learned about the weather, they have developed understandings about discussing and reporting the weather. As they have learned about going to see the doctor, they have learned what they will read there, what forms they will fill out, and about the kinds of information that medical personnel record. Children "are encultured into the most common and evident forms of [language and] literacy in their homes and communities before they even begin school" (Taylor 1997, 3). Language and literacy are sociocultural practices.

Varied Language Practices

Because family language and literacy practices vary greatly, each child's language and literacy enculturation is unique. Most families talk, read, and write as they run various errands in the community and do household tasks such as cooking, cleaning, and sorting through the mail, but families' ways of using language, and specific activities, differ. For example, some families actively include their children in daily literacy events; some encourage their children to observe more than participate. Some families use lots of oral language with their children; others enculturate more through modeling and demonstration.

Some families are always enjoying books of some sort; depending on their genre preferences, they may regularly share informative passages or captivating story lines. Some families read Chinese, Spanish, or English newspapers daily; they may share disturbing news about national events or funny lines from the comic strips. Some families receive lots of mail; they may cry or laugh over email from family members in Argentina, Greece, or Russia, and react to receiving junk mail and bills by wincing or throwing up their arms. Some families regularly read religious materials such as the Bible, the Koran, or daily devotions— some families read these in languages other than English. Some families participate in cultural events such as concerts, festivals, powwows, religious meetings, family celebrations, picnics, or community leadership activities, and share the literacy materials associated with these experiences. Some families enculturate their children into the kinds of language and literacy practices that will help them adjust to the routines and discourses of kindergarten; they read storybooks together, write together, and engage in adult-child question/answer exchanges much like those seen in classrooms.

As children experience these daily language and literacy practices, they develop cultural knowledge, including understandings about the literacies that are associated with that knowledge. Any time we read, write, or speak, we are using a specific form of language fit to and for specific social practices (Gee 1999). It is not surprising, then, that children as young as two and three begin to sort out the ways in which different language forms are used. For example, depending on their experiences, they discover that written language in newspapers looks and sounds different from written language on a grocery list; written language in storybooks is different from written language in nonfiction books. The oral language used by a priest or rabbi sounds different from that used by a teacher, coach, or newscaster. The language used by a store clerk sounds different from that used by a plumber or an electrician. Christian's students demonstrated their understandings about using varied language practices: as doctors they discussed patients' injuries using a serious, down-to-business register (Time 3:00); as newscasters, they reported the weather with an upbeat, slightly exaggerated register that included exclamations and adjectives (I mean hot!; very sunny; little tornado problem).

Throughout the early childhood years, each child develops a range of language forms suited to meet a range of social practices. Because of their varied experiences, the range varies from child to child. The results are that children come to school with very different knowledge and ready to learn in very different ways. Teachers who value such diversity encourage children to regularly share their knowledge in the classroom to extend their social learnings.

Varied Evaluation Practices

Given that language use differs from child to child, it makes sense to tailor evaluation to

connect with individual children's strengths. As we demonstrate, teachers accomplish this by collecting evaluation data as children engage in a variety of meaningful, authentic learning experiences, and by connecting with families. Learning about children's social and cultural experiences gives insights into their ways of speaking, knowing, and thinking. The task of the kidwatcher is to move toward a social-contextual approach in which evaluation involves understanding, valuing, and actively making use of each child's language and literacy.

Figures 2–1, 2–2, 2–3, and 2–4 provide ideas to help kidwatchers begin the social-contextual evaluation process. The items on these forms are designed to tap into parents'

Dear _____,

This information is most helpful to me as I get to know _____ and you. Please send it at your earliest convenience. Thank you. (Use the back, if needed.)

1. What changes (health, maturity, interests) have occurred in your child's life this summer?

2. What areas of school life has your child especially enjoyed? (Or, what areas do you anticipate your child will enjoy?)

3. Toward what areas of school life has your child expressed negative feelings?

4. What does your child do well?

5. What goals do you have for your child this year?

6. In general, how is your child's self-concept? Does he/she believe in his/her abilities?

7. What special needs (academic, social, personal, linguistic) does your child have?

8. Where does your child go after school?

9. What are your child's favorite after-school or weekend interests and activities?

10. What else do you want me to know about your child or about you?

Adapted from Howard (1994)

Reproducible, see p. 97

FIGURE 2–1   Getting to Know Your Child

Dear _____,

This information will help me get to know_____ and you. Please return it at your earliest convenience. Thank you. (Use the back, if needed.)

1. What are some of the things your child likes to do and talk about?

2. What are some places your child visits frequently?

3. In what settings does your child talk most comfortably?

4. What language(s) does your child speak? What language(s) are spoken in your home? Does your child hear different languages at family gatherings or in the community?

5. Do you ever read with your child or other children at home?

6. What different languages do family members read and write?

7. What kinds of reading does your child participate in alone or observe at home? In what languages?

8. List any of the family's favorite books, authors, characters, cartoons, or videos.

9. Does your child ever read TV advertisements or captions?

10. Does your child ever use or play on a computer?

11. What are some things your child likes to write or draw when given a blank piece of paper? What other kinds of writing does your child do?

12. What kinds of reading or writing do you and other family members like to do?

Reproducible, see p. 98

FIGURE 2–2   Getting to Know Your Child's Language and Literacy Practices

Child's Name: _____ Date_____ Grade _____

Please tell me about your child's language learning in the following areas, and share examples where possible. If more than one language is spoken in your home or family, please include information about which language you are referring to. I appreciate your insights as we work together with your child.

My Child:	Usually	Sometimes	Rarely	Comments and Examples (If more than one language is spoken, let me know about your child's strengths in each.)
Speaks clearly so others can understand				
Is able to follow oral directions				
Enjoys listening to and telling stories				
Enjoys being read to				
Has favorite books, characters, magazines				
Understands stories we read aloud				
"Reads" to me (telling about pictures and/or the story)				
Helps with grocery lists, coupons, shopping, recipes, and so on				
Tries to read words in real contexts and settings (street/store signs, cereal boxes)				
Draws pictures and writes some letters				
Writes in invented spelling (makes up spellings for words)				
Likes to tell about what he/she writes				

At home my child enjoys:

I have questions about:

Parent_____

Adapted from Language Arts Committee, Palo Alto Unified School District (1994)

Reproducible, see p. 99

FIGURE 2–3   My Child as a Language Learner: Parent Observation (Pre-K–1)

perspectives on their children's language learning. Whenever possible, personalize such forms by using the names of children and family members. Rather than using all the forms at once, choose just one, or use one early on and another later in the year. The items may be distributed to parents in the form of the questionnaires provided, discussed over the phone, or discussed in a face-to-face conference. Another possibility is to adapt and use the ideas as guidelines for note taking. Figure 2–5 (on page 20) provides a set of interview questions to be used with children, particularly, to gain insights into their reading and writing interests and attitudes. These ques-tions may be posed to children individually, in small groups, or as a class, with responses being recorded through anecdotal notes.

Language and Identity

As they inquire into children's home language and literacies, kidwatchers consider the role of identity in language learning. Children's identities develop under the influence of language, culture, race, class, gender, family values, patterns of domestic organization, and political, social, and religious ideology. Each of these becomes a characteristic of each child's identity. Children bring these characteristics to each literacy event. For example,

Child's Name: _____ Date_____ Grade _____

Please tell me about your child's language learning in the following areas, and share examples where possible. If more than one language is spoken in your home or family, please include information about which language you are referring to. I appreciate your insights as we work together with your child.

My Child:	Usually	Sometimes	Rarely	Comments and Examples (If more than one language is spoken, let me know about your child's strengths in each.)
Initiates and enjoys conversations with friends and adults				
Listens and responds appropriately to others				
Follows multistep directions				
Enjoys listening to and telling stories				
Enjoys being read to				
Has favorite books, characters, magazines				
Chooses to read independently				
Tries to read unknown words using meaning (good guesses), picture cues, or sounding out				
Can retell a story in own words				
Checks out books from school and public libraries				
Chooses to write independently (stories, poems, notes, lists, signs)				
Likes to talk about/share his/her writing				
Uses invented and correct spellings				

At home my child enjoys:

I have questions about:

Parent_____

Adapted from Language Arts Committee, Palo Alto Unified School District (1994)

Reproducible, see p. 100

FIGURE 2–4   **My Child as a Language Learner: Parent Observation (Grades 2–3)**

when some children (mostly the girls) in Christian's weather center regularly choose the quiet, behind-the-scenes roles, and others (mostly the boys) choose to be the hardy, robust reporters, identity is a likely catalyst. When one child says, "I can't write," and another says, "I can," identity is a likely catalyst. When one child says, "I don't like school," and another says "I do," identity is a likely catalyst. Identities guide children's behaviors, and therefore their development, by shaping their motivations, goals, purposes, attitudes, values, and ways interacting with print.

When kidwatchers evaluate, they consider the role that identity plays in children's demonstration and construction of knowledge. For example, if a child behaves in a seemingly unorthodox way during group in-

struction (is reluctant to speak; speaks constantly; begins to wander the room; stares downward), kidwatchers think about the forces that may be contributing to such a response. They know that, for a multitude of personal and cultural reasons, children have very different orientations toward school discourses. Some children are not comfortable with public performance; some are not comfortable drawing attention to themselves; some are not comfortable appearing to know more than their peers; and some are not comfortable talking extensively in front of adults. Any child may interpret interruptions differently than the teacher, have different ways of contributing to topics, be familiar with different patterns of turn taking, or have different understandings about the nature of questioning and response (Lindfors 1991). When children's ways "bump into" school ways, kidwatchers ask themselves some questions:

1.   Why is the child responding this way; what are the possible reasons?
2.   How do I refine my teaching to establish stronger connections with the child's interests/strengths/needs/language practices/literacy practices/social world?
3.   How do I support the child in expanding his/her interests/strengths/language practices/literacy practices in order to extend/support learning in the school setting?

Taking thoughtful action on issues of identity is not a simple task because identity is so deeply ingrained in the fabric of our selves and our social interactions. Even to the most knowledgeable teachers, it is not always clear why children do the things they do. Taking stock of the issues to consider is a good way to begin. When teachers ponder the social and cultural forces that shape children's identities, they can begin to take into consideration the ways in which the specific elements of these forces influence learning in the classroom. As teachers observe children and document information provided by families, their understanding of pertinent identity-related issues grows.

Reading
1. Do you like to read? Why or why not?
2. What do you like to read?
3. Why do people read?
4. What do you read at home?
5. Who do you read with?
6. Do people in your family read anything in languages other than English?
7. Do you read a language other than English?
8. What are your favorite books? Cartoons?
9. When you have lots of books to choose from, how do you decide which to read?
10. Who is a good reader you know? What makes that person good?
11. Do you read TV ads or captions?
12. Do you play computer or video games?

Writing
13. Do you like to write? Why or why not?
14. What do you like to write?
15. Do you like to draw when you write? Would you rather draw before or after you write? Why?
16. How do you decide what to write about?
17. Why do people write?
18. What do you write at home?
19. Who do you write with?
20. Do people in your family write anything in languages other than English?
21. Do you write in a language other than English?
22. Do you send letters or cards to others?
23. If you could choose one thing to write about, what would it be?
24. Who is a good writer you know? What makes that person good?

Experiences That Inform Reading and Writing
25. What kinds of things do you like to do?
26. What do you do well?
27. What are you curious about/what would you like to learn about?
28. What is something important you have learned?
29. How do you learn at school? At home?

Interpretive Questions for the Teacher
- What are the child's attitudes toward reading and writing?
- What are the child's preferences when it comes to reading and writing?
- What are the child's home experiences with reading and writing?
- What knowledge does the child have about language functions/sociocultural uses?
- How can I support children in bringing familiar language and cultural experiences to the school setting and using them to extend their knowledge?

FIGURE 2–5   **Finding Out What Kids Think**

Equally as important as learning from individual children and families is for teachers to continue to more formally educate themselves about the language and cultural backgrounds of their students. This is accomplished through study groups with other teachers, attending and presenting at professional conferences, taking classes for professional development, and extensive reading. At the end of this chapter we have included a list of authors who have helped us understand social, cultural, and identity issues.

Organizing a Rich Environment for Learning

Cognizant of the tremendous impact of children's early enculturation, kidwatchers create learning environments in which school practices connect with children's personal and social worlds. Driving this is the understanding that children learn best when language and experiences are meaningful to them. That is why many teachers avoid requiring children to explore content that is far removed from their lives—such as Mesopotamia, the solar system, or prehistoric civilizations—unless a current event or children's avid inter-

ests make it relevant to their lives. And, that is why they avoid putting children through decontextualized literacy activities such as filling in blanks on tedious worksheets, copying teacher-chosen words from the chalkboard, or studying units of information to which they have no prior connection. "Students do not master any school practice without being motivated to enter into and identify with that practice and without believing that they will be able to function within it and use it now or in later life" (Gee 1999, 362). To effectively evaluate, teachers observe children as they engage in purposeful and meaningful language and literacy events.

Relevance, Ownership, and Choice

Learning in school is purposeful and meaningful when children (1) find the curriculum *relevant* to their personal and social worlds; (2) *own* their learning activities; and (3) make *choices* about what and how they will learn (K. Goodman 1986). Whether kidwatchers guide students through preestablished curricular topics or projects arising from their own interests, they allow for children's questions, interests, and ideas to drive the curriculum. Reasons to read emerge as children encounter real opportunities to wonder, question, and inquire. Reasons to write emerge as children gain new insights, decide to further explore a topic, and want to permanently record information. Reasons to talk emerge as children discover connections with their beyond-school knowledge, collaborate with others on projects, and want to share what they are coming to know. Whether children are inquiring into family life, communities, insects, or the weather, kidwatchers encourage them to make choices that take them down meaningful and purposeful paths. The kidwatching teacher plans for all children to expand their language knowledge, and knowledge about the world, by building upon existing knowledge and existing ways of knowing.

Family Connections

Teaming with families is another way to meaningfully expand the curriculum. As it becomes appropriate to the children's inquiries, teachers invite family members to come to school to share their *funds of knowledge* (Moll and Greenberg 1990), or the information, strategies, tools, and technologies they use to accomplish their daily tasks of living. These funds range from ways of solving a problem to ways of shopping smartly; from techniques for repairing a toy to techniques for composing a song; from methods of carving a bowl to methods of playing the dulcimer. Funds of knowledge "are not possessions or traits of people in the family but characteristics of people-in-an-activity." This means that they are not dispensed to children, but passed on through

scaffolded activities, becoming a memorable aspect of children's histories. "Within these activities much of the teaching and learning is initiated by the children's interests and their questions . . . [so that] knowledge is *obtained* rather than imposed by adults" (Moll and Greenberg 1990, 326).

Sharing knowledge need not be limited to classroom activity. Many children become involved in projects that take them into the home and community to purposefully collect information. For example, from their homes, they may be interested in collecting stories, oral histories, work-related information, or information about hobbies such as gardening, sewing, woodworking, or detailing cars. Within the community, children may document what they learn on a trip to the post office, beauty salon, gas station, or video shop, or, with parent guidance, they may arrange to interview a community worker they know. Connecting home, community, and classroom brings into being a curriculum that reflects the rich knowledge of the family and culture.

Whenever possible, teachers arrange for the funds of knowledge shared by family members to become a significant part of classroom practice. For example, if a great-grandfather demonstrates how he makes maple syrup, or an older sister shows her process of seeking employment, children have opportunities to explore this information in subsequent weeks through reading, writing, play, and hands-on activity. Rather than the sharing being a one-time event, with families popping in and out of classroom life, children are encouraged to engage in follow-up explorations, and family members are invited to act as consultants throughout the year. In this way, family contributions are substantive, shaping both the content and process of classroom learning (Moll and Greenberg 1990).

With each family contribution, adults help children tune into and make connections among the varied language and literacy practices associated with life in their families and communities. What emerges is a "community of practice" (Gee 2000) in which adults and children with varied kinds of expertise create, share, and pass on a culture of literacy. Children come to value the literacy of their homes, and the classroom community enriches the literacy practices of the children. Figure 2–6 provides an example of a form used to gain information about potential family connections. As you use the forms in this book, remember to select the ones that are most relevant to you at particular times during the year, and to adapt them to serve your particular goals.

Using Assessment Data

Systematically collecting information on the sociocultural aspects of children's literacies gives kidwatchers numerous insights for planning curriculum and instruction. Sociocultural information is collected through field notes, interviews, informal conversations, conferences, questionnaires, home-school journals, and work samples. Some of this takes place early in the year and some the teacher initiates later. The following questions provide a framework for thinking through and analyzing observations and contacts with families—and using them to create meaningful conditions for learning.

Home-Based Information

▶ What funds of knowledge are present in the child's home?

▶ What print materials are regularly used in the home?

▶ What kinds of literacy interactions and relationships does the child have with others in the household?

▶ What kinds of literacy interactions does the child have with friends and family in other settings?

▶ What is the child's language background?

▶ What is the child's cultural background?

▶ What goals and expectations does the family have for the child?

▶ What do family members recall about their own experiences with language and literacy in school settings?

Classroom-Based Information

▶ What topics/content/genres are of interest to the child?

▶ What language and literacy practices does the child lean toward when given a choice?

▶ How would I characterize the child's language and literacy identity?

▶ What discourse patterns seem familiar to the child?

To help make this school year meaningful for each child, we would like to invite family members to share their expertise with us. The following information will be useful as we plan the children's educational experiences for the school year.

What knowledge, guidance, or experiences would you like to offer to the classroom?

__ Work with children on projects (help them write, read, find information). Please let us know if you are able to support children in languages other than English.
__ Listen to children read. In which language? _____
__ Bring in a story to read. In which language? _____
__ Tell a story (personal, family, community, traditional, folktale).
__ Sing a song or play a musical instrument.
__ Share hobbies or work-related knowledge such as cooking, painting, car detailing, gardening, fishing, sewing, woodworking, secretarial, retail, and so on.
__ Share an object of interest from your home.
__ Demonstrate how you use technology in some part of your life.
__ Share a childhood game.
__ Teach about the languages you use.
__ I prefer to observe only.
__ Other_____

What sorts of home-school connection activities would you prefer?

__ Visiting the classroom during the school day.
__ Evening activities and workshops.
__ Child study groups (groups of parents discuss their children's learning).
__ Take-home activity packs.
__ Home-school journals (writing back and forth with the teacher).
__ Family-oriented homework (biographies, collecting family stories).
__ Personal notes or emails to and from the teacher.
__ Phone calls to and from the teacher.
__ Classroom newsletter.
__ Communication in languages other than English: _____
__ Other_____

Does anything make it difficult for you to participate in school activities?

__ Dates and times of school activities.
__ Conflicts with work.
__ Not comfortable speaking the language(s) spoken in the school.
__ Younger children at home (or others who may need care).
__ Not enough information (about the activities, dates, times).
__ Other _____

Your Child's Name: _____

Adapted from Owocki (2001)

Reproducible, see p. 101

FIGURE 2–6   Families in the Classroom

▶ How is the child applying familiar language and literacy practices to new contexts and settings?

▶ What themes and roles does the child explore in play? How are language and literacy used in play?

Child-Based Information

▶ What are the child's views of himself/herself as a reader and writer?

▶ What is the child interested in learning/reading/writing about?

▶ Which kinds of reading, writing, and collaborative experiences does the child prefer?

▶ What is the child learning about himself/herself as a learner?

▶ How does the child feel about school?

Community-Based Information

▶ What family-oriented agencies are present in the community?

▶ What shopping facilities and other businesses are present in the community (small grocery stores or large supermarkets; clothing stores)? What kinds of foods and merchandise are available?

▶ What signs are present in the community? What is the language of the signs?

▶ What libraries, bookstores, and shops with magazines are available to families?

▶ What places of historic interest are present in the community?

▶ How diverse are housing patterns and the population in terms of age, race, ethnicity, and family structures?

Teachers who kidwatch from a sociocultural perspective actively consider the ways in which their own frames of reference influence their data analysis. Because cultural understandings and perspectives are often implicit (not recognized on a conscious level),

this takes a concentrated effort. To some extent, we are all trapped within our own views of the world; we respond to the world from our own perspectives. As teachers, we do not need to try to eclipse these perspectives; we just need to examine the ways in which our own positions affect our decision making in the classroom and to continue to develop a multicultural perspective. To facilitate this process, we recommend reading and collaborating with other teachers. As you do so, you may find it helpful to discuss and perhaps write out your thoughts on your choice of the following questions:

Questions for Teacher Self-Reflection

▶ What is my definition for *literacy*?

▶ What do my own literacy practices look like? What literacy materials are in my home, and what do they tell about me as a literate individual?

▶ How do my views of literacy influence my organization of the classroom; what I teach; how I teach; my interactions with students; my data gathering; my data analysis?

▶ What kinds of literate behaviors do I value over others? Where do these values come from? In what ways do these values limit the frames of reference from which my students may approach their learning? In what ways do they expand my students' frames of reference?

▶ What social hierarchies are present in my classroom? Who gets to be in charge of activities? When and why? Who works and plays together? What kinds of social interactions occur during work and play? Who leads? Who is left out? Are the social hierarchies connected with language and literacy?

▶ Am I providing materials, conditions, and experiences that allow all of my students to explore, expand, and value their existing literacies?

► What literacies does the school culture promote over others? How can I influence this?

Observing and documenting children's varied language and literacy practices, while making a conscious effort to think about your own frames of reference, helps you capitalize on pathways of learning that may otherwise go undiscovered. In our view, it is without question that all children need access to many different kinds of literacies, and all need to develop competence in the language and culture of the school, but this need not occur at the expense of any child's identity. An identity of competence develops as teachers provide instruction that is grounded in meaningful cultural experiences, and as children are gently supported in walking on familiar ground as they explore new literacies.

Transcending the Politics of Literacy and Schooling

Sadly, many children's literacies are threatened, rather than valued and expanded, in school settings. A major threat lurks in the political and institutional discourses that often mold curriculum and instruction. What counts as literacy in politics and institutions is often that which can be measured on tests, that which can be studied in a prepackaged sequence, and/or that which has been defined by the dominant culture as worth knowing. What often does not count is children's ability to negotiate written language within and across a variety of situations and to interpret and construct whole texts within meaningful social settings. There are teachers, who for fear of falling short on test scores, or because the underlying message from the institution is that a predetermined curriculum is best for children, find it daunting to move into new evaluation practices. On top of this, their own enculturation has led to their current understandings of what school is and should be like. If schooling (which worked well enough for the teacher) involved studying a curriculum presented in textbooks, following it in

an orderly sequence, and being tested on that curriculum, then this may have created the perception that this is all that school can, or needs to, be for children. It may also feel like a safe way to teach.

The result of political and institutional discourses, and unexamined personal ideologies, is a static curriculum designed to connect primarily with the literacy practices of children who are deemed "ready" for school. Typically, but not always, these are white, middle-class children who have learned to do things such as read and retell the stories in books, recognize and write the letters of the alphabet, write their names, and talk and act like "students." Such a curriculum is not designed to connect with the children who have been encultured into similarly valuable, but not-so-school-like practices. "Arguably, one of the principal reasons poor and minority children fail more often [than white, middle-class children] in school is that they face the challenge of mastering the *unfamiliar*, while their more successful peers practice the *familiar*" (Murphy and Dudley-Marling 2000, 381). Defining literacy based on political or institutional discourses, or even a teacher's personal discourses, limits access to learning for all children but particularly for those whose literacies differ vastly from those of the dominant culture. Such practices pull our teaching away from children's lived literacies and push it toward predetermined sets of goals or standards—those set by individuals who are far removed from classrooms and who, often, are working with agendas that may not be in the best interest of particular students. Such practices deny children the legitimacy of their own experiences and of using them to learn.

We encourage you to take a different approach. Interrupt this process by embracing a sociocultural pedagogy that values all children's literacies. Keep your eyes open to what all of your students know and can do. Search your ways of thinking for inconsistencies and biases. Join hands with other teachers in your district who are asking tough questions and critically examining their ways of viewing children. Join hands with teachers across the country who are standing up and saying, "I know. I am an expert. I am capable of making my own teaching decisions." Join hands with families, because with them, teacher voices are stronger. Do it for children, and be a positive force in a society's struggle toward equity. Do it for yourself, and enjoy the intellectual challenge of treading new ground.

Building a Community of Practice

Children's lives are filled with language and literacy. Delicately they come into your classroom with myriad kinds of knowledge and ideas, each having the potential to connect them with new knowledge, new ways of knowing, other children, and you. A strong web of classroom literacy grows as, with each day, teachers and children capture opportunities to expand their developing competencies and make learning connections with one another. The literacy web grows as children have the power to use written language at school as they do in home and community settings. The web grows as children and their families discover that what counts as reading and writing at home, counts as reading and writing at school. It is within a caring and warm "community of practice" (Gee 2000) that children develop multiple literacies, and identities as competent learners and communicators.

More Information About Sociocultural Knowledge and Experience

Following are some of the references we consult to understand diversity in language and literacy practices:

Home- and Classroom-Based Studies

Anne Dyson (1989)

Vivian Gussin Paley (1997)

Denny Taylor (1983; 1988)

Melanie Uttech (1997)

Shirley Brice Heath (1983)

Susan Phillips (1983)

Kelleen Toohey (2000)

Kathryn Whitmore and Caryl Crowell (1994)

Theoretical Pieces (any by these authors)

Barbara Comber
Paulo Freire
James Gee
Kris Gutiérrez
Sonia Nieto
M. A. K. Halliday

Gloria Ladson-Billings
Judith Lindfors
Jeannie Oakes
Lev Vygotsky
Luis Moll

Print Awareness

Aaron (22 months) sees a Burger King coffee cup and says, "I want French fries, mommy."

Patti (30 months) points to the writing on the cup she uses for lunch at preschool. (Her name is written on it.) "What's this say? It says, *My Lunchbox.*"

Children are steeped in encounters with people who use written language in all aspects of their lives. Because they want to participate socially in the same events as their loved ones, they become curious about print and begin to experiment with reading and writing. By the time most children enter school, they already have a good sense of how written language is used in their worlds, and have already begun to make discoveries about important print concepts. A smart way for early childhood educators to begin the school year, therefore, is with an assessment of children's print awareness.

Print Awareness: Some Developmental Moments

Children who are *aware* of print know that it is something significant and worth paying attention to. These children, whether through environmental print, shared writing, storybooks, or alphabet books, have tuned in to written symbols and begun to recognize their shapes and forms. In the earliest phases of print awareness, most children come to understand that letters can be named. Some learn to name all the letters. But perhaps more exciting is the point at which children recognize that letters have the potential to communicate. When young children point to print and ask, "What does that say?" or when they write a few letterlike shapes and call out, "This says *Mama!*" they are demonstrating the understanding that print involves an act of meaning. Reading begins at this point of awareness.

Understanding What Symbols Mean

Once children develop the understanding that alphabetic symbols carry meaning, they begin to hypothesize about what those symbols can mean. For the youngest children, of course, reading is not alphabetic. In other words, they do not yet know that symbols relate to sounds. For example, when twenty-two-month-old Jacob points to *any* print, he reads it either as *Jacob* or *STOP*. He knows that print "means," but he hasn't yet developed the understanding that letters in English relate to sounds to make up words. When predicting what the print says, he chooses words he has heard his family read often.

As children gain more experience, they become more sophisticated at negotiating the cues from the visual display. This becomes clear when observing a child reading print in a meaningful situational context, such as on a toothpaste tube or colorful book cover. Three- and four-year-old readers commonly use colors, pictures, shapes, and textures to predict what the print might say. That is why we often see them doing things like hypothesizing that the large print on a Crest tube says toothpaste, or that the print on the cover of a book says *lion* (the animal pictured on the cover). Early on, it is typical for children to predict that print functions as some sort of label (often a noun) that names the object or contents. Over time, they discover that print can do more than label. It can also describe objects and tell what they do (Ferreiro and Teberosky 1982).

With experience, children learn which aspects of the visual display are most significant for communication and become more selective in their use of cues. Colors and textures become less a focus as children come to understand that readers focus on the print. However, the important questions for the youngest readers seem to be "What is written language for?" and "What does it mean?"

Understanding How Symbols Mean

Children eventually begin to test hypotheses not only about what alphabetic symbols can mean but also about how they mean, or how they are organized. Because many children are not yet alphabetic at this point (they don't know that letter patterns systematically relate to sounds), they make hypotheses that are based on the visual aspects of words, or on how they look (Schickedanz 1999). In this book, we focus mostly on how children come to know features of alphabetic languages, such as English and Spanish. Children immersed in languages such as Chinese and Japanese make alternative hypotheses based on the organization of the written languages of their cultures and societies. As language learners in an English-dominant society, these children develop hypotheses about multiple languages.

Size and Length

As they work to discover how symbols mean, some children hypothesize that long strings of letters (PANOBOB) are used to represent big things, like *barn* or *granddaddy* while short strings of letters (BMD) are used to represent small things, like *salamander* or *Rebecca*. This makes sense considering that in pictures and real life, barns are bigger than salamanders and granddaddies are bigger than little girls

(Gundlach 1982). Heaviness, length, and age are other criteria that have been observed to play a part in the number or size of letters children use to represent objects (Ferreiro and Teberosky 1982).

Unique Designs

Another common visually based hypothesis is that letters belong to people, places, or things. For example, two-year-old Zada reads the word *Zoo* as her own name. Rather than understanding that the Z makes the first sound in her name, she sees Z-A-D-A as a unique signature that represents, or belongs to, her (Schickedanz 1999). Although Zada has not yet discovered the alphabetic principle, she has reached an exciting milepost. In reading *Zada* for *Zoo*, she shows that she is beginning to attend not only to pictures, colors, and textures but also to the looks of the words themselves. Children who attend to words eventually realize that relatively few letters (only twenty-six in English) are used over and over to create all of the words in alphabetic languages. Zada will learn that the letter Z can be used to spell her name, as well as *zoo*, and the name of her classmate, *Zia*.

The Concept of Word

As children gain more information about written language, they develop more sophisticated hypotheses about what makes a word a word. They start to notice that words are a certain length, and that they have internal variation (no repeating of a letter more than twice in a row) (Ferreiro and Teberosky 1982; Schickedanz 1999). Words can only be words if they look a certain way. Even very young children begin to realize that written symbols have conditions that make them interpretable.

When children are first exploring words, they may not grasp that they must look different if they are to say different things. For example, one day at preschool, Carlos wrote a sign (using invented characters) and read it aloud: "No Girls Allowed in My Bedroom." When his teacher asked if the sign would apply to his mother, Carlos revised the meaning without changing the writing: "It says, 'No Girls Allowed Except My Mom.'"

Over time, children begin to hypothesize that if words are going to say different things, they must look different. In fact, when writing, if they don't know many letters, they may solve the problem by changing the order of those they know to make them look like different words (Ferreiro and Teberosky 1982; Ferreiro 1990). For example, Aster wrote and read aloud the following:

Written	Read
P R i W	Pencil
R P i	Paper
P E I O	Envelope

Aster understands that graphic differences support different intentions. She uses her current stock of ten or twelve letters to write anything she wants to say.

Directionality

As adults, we automatically read narrative (in the English language) from left to right, top to bottom. Directionality is not so obvious to young children, who may attempt to read (or write) right to left, or in a zigzag pattern, or even bottom to top (as indicated by their finger pointing). Another important early discovery, then, is that print (in English and Spanish) is read from left to right, top to bottom. Children immersed in written languages such as Chinese, Hebrew, and Arabic discover that some languages are written from right to left or vertically. Teachers need to document and take into consideration children's varied literacy experiences, especially when they ask children to "look at the first letter" or "write the first sound you hear."

Correspondence Between Oral and Written Language

Another important early discovery is that written messages relate in specific ways with oral language. As part of their early hypothesis testing, hearing children begin to play around with the ways in which oral and written language are related. For example, while playing restaurant, Karla wrote four lines of invented symbols, then read them aloud while pointing to each line with her finger: "Eggs and . . . bacon and . . . sal . . . ad." Karla understands that there is a correspondence between speech and written language. So, when she reads, she matches her voice to the print. To leave a line of print hanging would leave her in a state of cognitive conflict (Ferreiro and Teberosky 1982). Her temporary hypothesis helps her maintain a sense of equilibrium as she works toward conventional understandings.

Understanding How Letters Relate to Sounds

Eventually, children recognize that there is a relationship between letters and sounds (they become *alphabetic*), and begin to integrate visual with sound-based hypotheses. It is at this point that a child might recognize that C-R-E-S-T could not spell *Toothpaste* because "it starts with C." As they read, alphabetic children begin to focus more strategically on print cues than they did in their earlier days. Because all along they have experienced print in meaningful contexts, they are not left to using print alone to decide what an unknown word says. For example, when Christopher encountered the word *minestrone* on a soup can, he pointed to the word and said, "Mm-mm-i-my-mine . . . Oh! Minestrone!" First, the context of the can provides clues to what the print might say. The picture looks like it could be vegetable or minestrone, but certainly not tomato or chicken. Second, like all readers, Christopher draws on his background knowledge and vocabulary. He has eaten minestrone and used that term before. Third, because Christopher expects what he reads to make sense, he sees reason to work from his approximation to an accurate pronunciation. He is flexible enough to keep trying until he generates a sensible word choice.

Children who believe print will be meaningful can be expected to actively and flexibly explore ways of translating letters and letter patterns into sounds and sound patterns. Be-cause words are not spelled as they sound, children sometimes come up with an approximate pronunciation at first. Because the context provides clues, and because readers draw on background knowledge and vocabulary, they have information that helps them come up with a sensible word choice. At five, Christopher is just beginning to explore the alphabetic principle as he sorts out how letters match to sounds.

Over time, children become increasingly sensitive to letter-sound relationships and to the more complex phonics patterns found in words (such as -in; -ate; -ight; -ay). For example, Lexy's writing changed in the following ways during the fall of her first-grade year. First, she explored a syllabic hypothesis, as many children do. These children hypothesize that a spoken syllable corresponds with each written symbol:

I	went	to	Myr	tle	Bea . . .		ch
I	W	T	M	T	B		H

Lexy's example shows that while she was exploring a syllabic hypothesis, she was also exploring an alphabetic hypothesis. She was figuring out how letter patterns match to speech sounds. As the year went on, she began to represent more specific units of sound and to internalize the spellings of some commonly used words.

This	is	a	pic	ture	of	me	play	ing	soc	cer.
FS	IS	A	P	HR	F	ME	PA	E	SA	G

Toward December, she was conventionally spelling words she used frequently and generating more sophisticated inventions for unfamiliar words.

I	went	to	preschool	and	I	went	to	kindergarten.
I	want	to	PrscaL	and	I	wen	to	KnaGart

Throughout the early childhood years, as children continue to refine their alphabetic hypotheses, they continue to negotiate and integrate the various cues provided by text. Their development as readers is characterized by their gaining control over multiple cueing systems.

Before we move on, it is important to note that some children linger in certain phases of development longer than others, and sometimes the knowledge children demonstrate depends on the task at hand. For example, Tina is a first grader who is exploring the alphabetic principle, but one day during play, she used scribble marks to fill out a library card. At that moment, exploring the general function of a library card was more the focus for her than working through the spellings for each word. In tracking children's development of print awareness, kidwatchers keep in mind that the situational context may influence children's demonstrations of knowledge, and that maturation and sociocultural experiences vary from child to child. Children develop in their own directions, at their own rates, in their own social environments. Because of children's diverse interests, experiences, histories, and language, there are no standard steps that every child grows through.

Guidelines for Evaluation

As kidwatchers, we can think of no better way to sensitively teach all children than to start by taking stock of what each child knows, and then using that information to plan instruction and curriculum that help them grow from there. Taking stock of students' print awareness, both formally and informally, helps you profile and understand each student's

▶ knowledge about the print in the local environment (possibly including that which is written in languages other than English)

▶ hypotheses about what and how symbols mean

▶ understandings of written language functions

▶ understandings of written language features, including graphic characteristics, letter-sound relationships, and phonics

▶ views of self as a reader/author/literate individual

Although print awareness evaluations are primarily used with younger readers, they may also be appropriate for learners of any age who are insecure with or inexperienced in their interactions with print. The information gained from such evaluation identifies specific strengths of individual students and helps develop purposeful learning experiences.

Informal Print Awareness Evaluation

In preschool and kindergarten classrooms, informal evaluation of children's print awareness occurs on a daily basis. The basic procedures for informal evaluation involve setting up learning situations for children to informally transact with print, and taking field notes to document their language and actions. As you take notes, the following kidwatching questions will help you focus on key information:

1. What does the child know about print?
2. What evidence is there that print awareness is developing?
3. When a child produces something unexpected or unconventional, what does it tell about the child's knowledge?

Considering these questions helps you plan instruction and activities that are within your students' zones of proximal development (Vygotsky 1978), or that connect with what children already know and challenge them into new directions. Following are examples of ways to set up informal situations that enrich the curriculum and at the same time promote children's development.

Print from Home. Invite children to bring in pieces of environmental print they can read. A note to families explaining the purpose of the activity facilitates this process (see Figure 3–1). Either in small groups or whole-class settings, plan enough time for children to read and converse about the materials they have brought. Such a process sends the message to children and their families that you value the literacy events and

Dear _____,

Please join us! The children are making a collection of print they can read, and we need at least five pieces of environmental print from every child. What print in the environment is familiar to your child? Does he or she recognize any of the words on cereal boxes, cookie packages, fast-food containers, book covers, magazine covers, newspapers, traffic signs, local business signs, catalogs, coupons, advertisements, or toys? Please send in five items containing print that is familiar to your child. The print may be in languages other than English. We don't need the whole box, package, or container, just the part containing familiar print.

Thank you,

_____

FIGURE 3–1   Note to Families

experiences that occur in their homes. Discussing materials from home provides children with opportunities to articulate their understandings, and makes space for them to share their home culture. Because children can easily assume leadership of this activity, your time is freed for note taking.

Environmental Print Walks.   Take environmental print walks in the school, neighborhood, or community. Encourage children to point out the print they see, to discuss what they think it says and how they know, and to determine what purpose it serves in the school or community. If desired, carry chalkboards, clipboards, or notepads, and invite children to record any print they find interesting.

Photo Shoots.   Arrange for your children to participate in a photo shoot of the print in your school, neighborhood, or community. Each child points out print of interest, and adults are responsible for taking the pictures. Photographs are placed in an album. The date of the event is recorded, and a caption is dictated by the children. As you take field trips and further walks, continue to update the album. As the students revisit the albums throughout the year, they discover their own literacy development. Encourage families to develop photo albums of family experiences and to involve their child in selecting, labeling, and dating the pictures. These become delightful opportunities for families to read together, or for the child to share family experiences with peers at school.

Print Scrapbooks.   In partnership with children and their families, construct a scrapbook of print your students can read. Seek help from family members in collecting authentic items from homes (including print in languages other than English), and also arrange for children to browse magazines, catalogs, and newspapers.

Print Displays.   Invite family members to work with their children to develop a print display that can be set up in the classroom or contained on a poster. Two to four families create their displays every week. Anything around the house that has words on it may be used, including print in languages other than English, and including material printed from a computer. Children and/or family members formally present the display to the class and leave it up for browsing. Encourage children to discuss the display with one another at appropriate times.

Word Study Centers.   Create an environmental print word study center. Paste real pieces of print to large note cards and laminate. To help children develop their knowledge of print functions (e.g., foods, traffic signs, store signs) and features (letter-sound relationships, spellings), invite them to work together to sort the cards in various ways: by uses; words they can read, first or last letters, or sounds they hear in the words. As children become adept at reading the print, make the activities more challenging by removing the colors and other surrounding cues, or by writing the words in a standard font.

Play.   Place authentic literacy materials in play centers and document how children use and talk about them. Include food packages, catalogs, traffic signs, store signs, restaurant signs, menus, receipts, coupons, maps, weight and height charts, pads of paper, and pencils. Be sure to include materials that are culturally relevant to the children.

Formal Print Awareness Evaluation

To more formally evaluate children's print awareness, carefully collect a set of print items that reflects elements of the popular culture of your local area. The sociocultural evaluation (Chapter 2) helps you know the kind of print that is important in students' lives, for example, tofu, tortilla, rice, or matzah packages. Print items may include real packaging, photographs, and drawings, or they may be cut from magazines and newspapers. Figure 3–2 provides examples of items to include. To ensure that the items reflect the language and culture of your students, invite parents to help develop the collection. It is not necessary to use the same set of items for each student. Approximately fifteen items should suffice.

Do not be concerned if some of the items you choose are not familiar to some of your students. The assessments are not used to compare children, or to count how many pieces of print they recognize. Instead, they are used to help you learn how your students respond to various kinds of print, both familiar and unfamiliar, and to discover the strategies they use to make meaning from it. If you find that most of the items in your collection are unfamiliar to any student, be sure to consult the data related to cultural items (Chapter 2), or to consult with the child's family members to learn more about the kinds of print materials they have in their environment.

General Procedures

For the formal evaluation children are asked to react to the print in its full visual context, and then one step removed from that context (without the colors and accompanying illustrations). Although this procedure is somewhat inauthentic, children seem to enjoy the individualized contact, and teachers find it useful because it quickly reveals important information for planning authentic instruction. General procedures are as follows:

Task 1:   *Reaction to Print in a Two-Dimensional Context*
Present the child with print in a context that is one step removed from its original situational context.

Examples: A cutout portion of a cereal box; a picture of a traffic sign; a hand-sketched name of a cartoon or video game (colors maintained); a toothpaste label; a magazine cutout of a store sign. Paste items on tagboard and laminate. These can be hole punched and put into a binder for an evaluation booklet for the teacher.

1. Milk	11. Toys
2. Cereal	12. Newspapers
3. Soup	13. Magazine Covers
4. Dry Goods (Beans, Rice)	14. Fast Foods
5. Baby Food	15. Major Retailers (Home Depot, Wal-Mart)
6. Soda (Pop)/Local Drinks	16. Automobile Logos
7. Laundry Detergent	17. Traffic Signs
8. Bar Soap	18. Telephone Sign
9. Toothpaste	19. School Sign
10. TV Show/Cartoon Character Name	20. Gas Station

FIGURE 3–2   Print Awareness Item List

Task 2: *Reaction to Print in Familiar Graphic Units*
Present the child with representations of familiar print that is devoid of the accompanying colors and textures, but that maintains the original font.

Examples: Black-and-white representations of Crest, McDonald's, Sesame Street, Batman, or Raisin Bran. Cut out, paste on tagboard, and laminate.

Task 3: *Reaction to Print in Standard Fonts*
Present the child with the same items used in Tasks 1 and 2, but written by hand or in a computer's standard font.

Depending on your students' knowledge, you may choose to implement only Tasks 1 and 2, or only Tasks 2 and 3. Tasks 2 and 3 may even be used with second- or third-grade children who are still developing their print awareness. Play around with the assessments to determine what works best for you and gives you the kinds of information you find useful.

Implementing the Tasks

Although the print items change from task to task (from the whole object to only the printed form), the general procedures for Tasks 1, 2, and 3 remain the same. Figure 3–3 is used as a guide for implementing the procedures for each task and for taking note of the children's responses. Before you begin, number the selected print items (1–15). Then do all the #1s on the form first, the #2s next, and so on.

Child's Name: ______________________	Date: __________
Introduction	
Ensure that the situation is comfortable for the student and then explain the procedures: *I have some things to show you, and I'd like you to tell me what you know about them.* Or, *I'm going to ask you some questions.*	
Note whether student has had previous experience with the item:	*Have you ever seen this before? Where?* 1____ 6____ 11____ 2____ 7____ 12____ 3____ 8____ 13____ 4____ 9____ 14____ 5____ 10____ 15____
Note student's response to the print:	*What do you think it is? What do you think it says?* 1____ 6____ 11____ 2____ 7____ 12____ 3____ 8____ 13____ 4____ 9____ 14____ 5____ 10____ 15____
Note reasoning behind student's response:	*How do you know? What makes you think so?* 1____ 6____ 11____ 2____ 7____ 12____ 3____ 8____ 13____ 4____ 9____ 14____ 5____ 10____ 15____
Note the part of the graphic display to which student is responding:	*What tells you that it says . . . ? Show me with your finger where it says . . .* 1____ 6____ 11____ 2____ 7____ 12____ 3____ 8____ 13____ 4____ 9____ 14____ 5____ 10____ 15____

Reproducible, see p. 102

FIGURE 3–3 Evaluating Print Awareness

Techniques for Questioning and Interaction

The print awareness procedures may be implemented with varying degrees of formality, and may be used in one-on-one situations or adapted for small groups or whole-group settings. Whether evaluating print awareness formally or informally, we have found certain techniques to be helpful in guiding the questioning and interactions:

1. Maintain a casual atmosphere. Children must feel comfortable if they are to take the risks necessary for showing what they know. If their previous experiences have taught them they must always be "right," they may be hesitant to respond. This will affect your ability to get an adequate picture of their knowledge. If a child does not respond, or responds with "I don't know," gently probe with "Take a guess," or "Pretend you're reading."
2. Keep in mind that when print displays become too unfamiliar or decontextualized, children no longer see them as meaningful,

and they may let you know by showing restlessness or impatience. Keep going only as long as you feel you are gaining useful information that will inform your instruction. Do not keep a child at a task if he or she is obviously tense or uncomfortable.

3.   Explain to the child that you are writing down what he or she says so that you can remember it later. If the child asks what you are writing, it's okay to tell! If a child asks, "Was I right?" keep in mind that miscues and inventions are not the same thing as mistakes. Children's early interpretations of print are expected to reflect invention, which means that there is always more than one potential right answer. You might say, "I'm interested in what you think," or "What do you think?"

4.   Develop the art of rephrasing and paraphrasing. When asking the questions, use our suggested language as a frame, but vary it to make it understandable to the child. You may find that different children respond better to different wording. Open-ended questions that begin with "What do you think . . . ?" or "How do you know . . . ?" help children articulate their ideas and make their thinking clear. In contrast, "Can you . . . ?" or "Do you know . . . ?" tend to lead to yes/no answers.

5.   If you are using the print awareness tasks for research purposes, be sure to ask all the questions for each item and make sure that the child points to items when requested. A tape recorder will help you to be thorough in your documentation.

6.   In administering the formal assessments, avoid providing the child with information such as "Have you seen this in your refrigerator?" or "Do you like to eat this?" Use the formal assessment to discover what the child can do without too many clues from you.

7.   Avoid referring to items as "pictures" or "words." Use terms such as "it" or "this" or "card." In this way, you leave room to discover the child's understanding and use of literacy terms.

8.   To avoid order predictability, randomize the order in which you present the items for Tasks 1–3.

Questions as a Basis for Analysis

Using a set of questions to analyze data provides a helpful guide for planning future instruction. Consider the following:

▶   What knowledge does the child demonstrate about the print in the local environment?

▶   What kinds of interactions does the child have with print? Does the child understand that letters can be named; that print carries meaning; that print relates to oral language; that we read pictures and print in different ways; that words are made up of letters; that patterns of letters represent patterns of speech; that written words represent spoken words; that spaces indicate boundaries between words?

▶   In what ways does the child's knowledge change from item to item or task to task?

▶   How does the child's knowledge change over time?

▶   What do the child's errors or miscues reveal about his/her knowledge? (See Chapter 6.)

▶   What happens to the child's reading when surrounding visual cues are reduced or removed?

▶   How does the child respond to print in languages (other than English) that are used in the child's family/the community?

▶   How does the child respond to the "How do you know . . . ?" questions?

▶   What does the child do when encountering unknown items, words, or phrases?

▶ What are the child's understandings about the functions of print?

▶ What does the child know about letter-sound relationships; about more complex phonic patterns?

▶ What are the child's apparent views of him/herself as a reader? (Consider positive self-statements, willingness to take risks, and security in terms of not knowing.)

▶ In which situations and settings does the child seem most comfortable expressing and constructing knowledge?

Assessment Data Uses

Three-year-old examining a McDonald's french fry bag: "I don't know what it is, but my mommy says it's not healthy."

Observing and documenting children's print awareness fosters effective teaching. First, it helps you relate curriculum to children's experiences. Knowing children's familiarity with environmental print helps you determine the kinds of literacy materials to include in the play area, the kinds of environmental print to use for instruction, and the kinds of writing children might find meaningful (signs, menus, food packages, books, magazines, and so on). Second, print awareness evaluation sheds light on children's ways of interacting with print, which helps you know how to individualize your instruction. For example, some children need a great deal of situational and contextual information; others need less because they are exploring alphabetic hypotheses. Some children may respond more easily to materials in Spanish than English; some may respond in more depth when engaged in informal (versus formal) print awareness activities. Finally, print awareness evaluation gives you a frame for documenting children's knowledge and growth. The information you collect is placed in the child's work folder and/or cumulative folder, and is shared with families and children. It may also be passed on to the child's future teachers.

Goal: Expanding Competencies

Children's lives are filled with written language. By the time they come to school, most have a broad understanding of the functions that written language serves, and many are beginning to make specific discoveries about how print is organized. Your role as a kidwatcher is to understand your students' awareness of print so that you can sensitively help them build upon their existing competencies. Sometimes, people who work in the field of education make the mistake of assuming that because children do not respond with conventional answers to their questions, or do not respond with interest to a preplanned curriculum, they have little print knowledge. This is a misconception. All children who come to school have complex systems of knowledge. They have developed a sense of the patterns and routines of daily life and of how print fits into those patterns and routines. They know how to observe and make sense of the world. They seek answers to their questions. They wonder. They imagine. They think. Your task as a kidwatcher is to discover what children know and to use that information to support them in developing and expanding their competencies as confident language learners.

Books and Book Handling

Chloe (age 2) selects *Mrs. Wishy-Washy* (Cowley 1999) from a low shelf in her preschool classroom. She sits cross-legged on a pillow and pretends to read the name of the author and illustrator. Then, turning to the first page of the story, she begins to move her finger horizontally along the print, expressively repeating the phrase, "She wished and wished; she wished-y wished."

As Chloe transacts with literature she loves, she demonstrates her many understandings

about books and book handling. At the age of two, she has already developed knowledge that is foundational to her ability to construct meaning: She examines a book's cover before reading it; identifies the author and illustrator; and skips over the first few pages to begin her reading where the story begins. She turns pages from left to right, reads lines of print from left to right, and uses both pictures and what she remembers from previous readings to construct a meaningful text. Perhaps most important, Chloe has discovered that books are full of people, places, objects, and events that she finds interesting and worth reading about.

Children's early experiences with books provide them with infinite information about why people read, how to handle books, and how print communicates. Teachers who carefully observe and document students' understandings equip themselves to provide instruction that draws from individual strengths and is tailored to meet individual needs. Part of kidwatching involves knowing what children know about books so that you can support them in building and extending their existing knowledge. We begin this chapter with a description of children's early book knowledge and how it develops, and then continue with guidelines and suggestions for evaluation.

Book-Handling Development

For many years now, teachers and researchers have been closely observing what children do and say when they transact with books. The major goals have been to find out how children handle books; how they learn about them; what aspects of the print and illustrations they attend to; and the meaning they construct. The results in general show that well before children begin to read conventionally, depending on their experiences, they develop knowledge about (1) the functions of books, (2) the routines used to share them, (3) the oral discourses used to discuss them, and (4) the concepts and strategies needed to construct a meaningful text. As you read, keep in mind that kidwatchers collect information in each of these areas so they know how to best help children build upon what they know already.

The Functions of Books

Five-year-old Michael awakens and ambles to the kitchen, where he hears dishes clinking. As he crawls onto a stool, he joins his sister Ivy, who is drinking tea and reading a mystery, his sister Piper, who is eating cereal and reading an Archie comic book, and his mother, who is drinking coffee and looking up a recipe for potato soup.

The most important discovery that young children make about books is that they serve meaningful functions. At five, Michael has already discovered that books do such things as entertain, provide information, satisfy curiosity, and offer pleasant moments of intimacy with other people. Michael's parents and older sisters have been reading books to him (and in his presence) almost daily since he was born. In such a setting, Michael has learned that books are worth paying attention to. The whole family reads *stories* because they find pleasure in doing so; Michael likes funny stories the best. The family uses *nonfiction* books for anything from learning how to play the piano to learning how to speak another language; from expanding their knowledge about the local environment to dreaming about faraway countries. Some of Michael's favorite nonfiction topics are sharks and dinosaurs. Michael's family members use recipe books for cooking, map books for traveling, professional literature for doing their jobs, and hobby-related books to support all kinds of activity. An important part of Michael's literacy enculturation involves his coming to know why and how the significant people in his world use books. Children who believe that books serve meaningful functions have reason to read them and reason to learn to read them. Teachers who understand how books function in their students' lives, and the level of value children place on books, have a head start in creating a learning environment that connects with children's personal worlds.

The Routines of Book Sharing

Another part of children's literacy enculturation entails developing knowledge of book-sharing routines. As children share books with others, they learn where to sit in relation to the book (on a lap or on the floor so they can see the pictures), how to participate, when to speak, and when to listen. For each child, book sharing is different. In home settings, children may become accustomed to sitting on laps for reading stories, all the while touching the book and talking about the pictures, words, letters, and interesting parts. Or, they may learn to listen more quietly, as others read not only from children's books, but also from recipe books, the newspaper, comic strips, or the Bible. Preschoolers in classroom settings, depending on the teacher's style, may learn to sit quietly while a teacher reads, or to chime in, comment, and ask questions whenever they wish. Children develop different book-sharing routines depending on the settings in which they read books and the interactional styles of the people with whom they read.

Children also learn to vary their ways of participating depending on the genre of the book. For example, at Under One Sun Desert School in Tucson, Arizona, teachers typically read storybooks all the way through as children look at pictures and occasionally ask questions or make comments. With nonfiction books, instead of reading straight through, the teachers talk more casually, asking questions of the children, pointing out interesting pictures, or requesting that children share what they know about the topic. With poetry and predictable big books, the children are encouraged to chant, sing, and read along when they can. Many children learn that the routines of book sharing change depending on the genre of literature.

The examples shared so far illustrate that by the time they are five, some children have developed complex concepts about the functions of books, and about the routines used to share them. Contrast this with the five-year-old who enters kindergarten having had very few experiences with books. This child may be willing to comply with the instructional practices surrounding books, but may not understand the purpose of sitting quietly with hands in lap or listening to what a teacher reads. The confusion may be exacerbated if the focus of an already-abstract task (reading) is on learning abstract bits of language, rather than on first learning to enjoy and appreciate literature. Not surprisingly, because instructional book experiences seem meaningless to some children, they may engage in disruptive, silly, or passive behaviors during shared book experiences.

Kidwatchers believe that all readers need sensitive and meaningful enculturation into the world of books. Regardless of the age at which children have their first experiences with books, we want them to be characterized by an emotional engagement that enables learning to happen. Children who are emotionally engaged enjoy listening to and reading books, and understand that literature can enhance, influence, and inform their lives. As you document book-handling behaviors in your classroom, keep an eye out for engagement, because that is what leads to children's being receptive to learning the language and literacy concepts needed for reading.

The Oral Discourses Surrounding Books

Three-year-old twins Madison and Noah are sitting on their Grandma Sue's lap for a bedtime story. "Noah," Sue requests, "would you turn the pages? I can't reach them and hold both of you at the same time."

Another part of children's literacy enculturation involves developing the oral discourses that are associated with talking about and learning from books. Book reading is always situated within particular language practices that shape both what and how children learn. Some preschool teachers and family members ask lots of questions and encourage a great deal of participation as they share books with children. Others encourage them to listen more quietly. Other adults stay mostly on the sidelines as children interact with books. Some children develop ways to participate in book reading through early experiences with storytelling. Along with family members, they may echo the language of the storyteller, interrupt to add their own experiences, and engage in numerous other acceptable cultural response forms. Because of their varied experiences, children's discourses differ.

Because most elementary school teachers use books for reading instruction, it is important that children learn appropriate discourses for exchanging information about books. One area of particular importance involves learning to use and respond to reading-related terms and phrases such as *What does that mean? What did you think about the ending? Which character did you like? Turn back one page. Read that first line again. Can you point to the words as I read? Where is the letter* C? Because of their years of experience, many children have a well-developed sense of these discourses by the time they are five. Their knowledge is important, considering that teachers use such discourses to scaffold children's literacy. Part of kidwatching involves taking note of the language children use to understand, respond to, and discuss books. This enables you to provide comprehensible instruction that is sensitive to your students' current knowledge, experience, and ways of knowing.

The Process of Constructing a Meaningful Text

Todd is holding his two-year-old son, Jake, on his lap. Together, they are reading *The Very Hungry Caterpillar* (Carle 1969):

TODD: On Monday, he ate one . . . What did he eat, Jake?
JAKE: Apple.
TODD: On Tuesday, he ate two . . .
JAKE: Pear.
TODD: On Wednesday, he ate three . . .
JAKE: Blue.
TODD: [*whispers*] Plums.
JAKE: Plums . . .

A final component of children's enculturation into books involves learning specific concepts and strategies that enable the construction of a meaningful text. Educators sometimes erroneously assume that when children can manipulate letters and sounds, they have developed the most important knowledge for

reading; yet, Jake's example illustrates that reading involves the simultaneous negotiation of multiple meaning-making strategies. Already, this two-year-old is learning to turn the pages of a book in the appropriate direction, to use pictures and prior knowledge to fill in parts of the story, and to make a correction when something doesn't make sense. Teachers observe and document children's conceptual and strategic knowledge as they engage in book-handling activity because it helps them monitor their growth and plan instruction based on their strengths. Specifically, they document children's

► sense of directionality

► ideas about what is significant from the visual display

► knowledge of literary forms

► knowledge of written language registers

► holistic remembering

► strategies for moving from print to meaning

Directionality

As children read, talk about, and observe others reading books, they develop a sense of the directionality of written language. Children with a fully developed sense of directionality in English have learned to do the following while handling a book:

► orient the book in its upright position

► turn the pages in the appropriate direction

► view the print on the left page before viewing the print on the right page

► read the lines of print from left to right, top to bottom

Children develop concepts of directionality at a very early age. An infant as young as seven or eight months may push a page in the appropriate direction after an adult has separated it from the remaining pages (Schickedanz 1999). By two, many children have learned to open books by themselves and turn pages in the appropriate direction (left to right in English and Spanish; right to left in Hebrew and Arabic). As evidence of their growing awareness of print (often around four or five), some children begin to move their finger along the lines of print as they turn through the pages of books, or point to labels as pictures are named. Eventually, they begin to do so in the appropriate direction for their language. Many teachers purposely introduce books with varied formats and layouts to expand students' repertoires of understandings about the directionality of print.

Determining Significance

Determining significance is another concept that children develop as they have experiences with written text. In Chapter 3 we pointed out that, as children read environmental print, they learn to sort out exactly which information from the visual display is significant to constructing meaning. The same holds true with books, magazines, and newspapers. Not all of the colors, pictures, or even words in a text are particularly helpful for meeting a reader's goals. For example, when opening a book, it is common for readers to skip over publishing information, interior title pages, and dedications. In magazines, readers often skip to the first article. With newspapers, readers often skip to the sections they find most interesting. When reading any kind of text, children must figure out which writing and which illustrations are significant to meeting their goals.

For young children, a major breakthrough in determining significance involves the discovery that the print carries the language of the story. Early on, when asked, "Where am I reading?" younger children often indicate that the pictures provide the language information, sometimes pointing to the mouth of the character. Before they enter first grade, most children discover that print and illustrations serve different functions. This seems to happen earlier and more often with children who are read to in one-to-one or small-group settings.

It is important to note that effective readers do not stop looking at pictures once they realize the significance of print. Eye movement research with first graders shows that children know the significance of both the print and the pictures and use them in concert with each other to construct their understanding of books. Six-year-olds pay more attention to print in books than they do to pictures (Duckett 2001).

Knowledge of Literary Forms

Knowledge of literary forms, the written language structures and grammars that authors regularly use, is another element of literacy that develops as children have experience with books and other literature. Children learn over time to distinguish between fiction and nonfiction in terms of both its content and its style. For example, children who listen to traditional *stories* learn that authors usually introduce characters (both likable and unlikable) and a setting, and then give the main character a problem that is eventually resolved. Children who listen to *nonfiction* become familiar with typical expository structures, such as definition and example, cause and effect, comparison and contrast, time order, and description. By listening to children's responses to books and to their oral (or pretend) reading, teachers gain insights into their knowledge of literary forms.

The way children use knowledge about form to construct a text may be both developmental and a reflection of their early experiences. At age three, many children *label* items and characters, and talk about the illustrations on each page as if they are independent entities—as if one illustration is unrelated to the next. At four and five, children move from labeling to describing what is happening, and they become increasingly sensitive to the connected sequences of events that happen across the pages of a book. Is this a developmental trend or is it a matter of experience?

Picture books containing labels rather than a connected discourse are usually among the first books families read to children. And, with younger children, adults often simplify the text to hold children's attention or make it understandable. Therefore, younger children's tendency to label may be partially due to the order and style in which adults present varying kinds of text. "Younger children talk about books in the ways they have heard books talked about . . . As they hear more actual stories, their talk becomes more like written language, and each page is treated as part of an overall story" (Schickedanz 1999, 82). Children's way of reading may also depend on the adult's way of requesting that they read. When prompted, "Tell me about this," the child may point to each page and each picture and respond by describing or labeling. When prompted, "Read me a story," the child will more often use a storytelling discourse. In general, however, we can say that over time, children's responses show evidence that they progressively build understandings about the content, as well as the macrostructure, or overall connective organization, of what they are reading.

Knowledge of Written Language Registers

Karla (age four) reads aloud a story she has written using invented symbols: "One morning, three curious cats and dogs got tooken to a wonderful place called animal control. They all got tooken in cages that early morning in the summer . . ."

Register is another language concept that helps children construct a meaningful text. Children who are read to learn that the language in books, newspapers, and magazines differs from the language we speak. Karla's use of literary language such as *One morning, three curious cats and dogs . . .* and *that early morning in the summer* shows that she is developing a written language register—a style and tone that is uniquely suited to written forms of language. Even though she invents written symbols for this piece, when she reads aloud, she sounds very much like an older child ex-

pressively reading a story. It is interesting that some children use a reading-aloud intonation even before they are using language that others can understand (Y. Goodman 1980; Schickedanz 1999).

Children develop a variety of written language registers as they hear adults read a variety of kinds of text. Eventually they begin to respond to a book in a way dependent on its genre, showing their understanding that language forms vary from book to book. For example, Karla's story in the opening vignette shows her sense of the language associated with fiction. When cues suggest the book is fiction, children may begin with "Once upon a time," "One morning," or "One day." If cues suggest nonfiction, their language is likely to reflect a nonfiction register. For example, while reading aloud from a dinosaur book, Karla said, "Tyrannosaurus Rex bones . . . We lock them up, and we dig for them with shovels and hammers and plungers. We roll it on the trucks, and we carry them to the museum . . . We put the bones together. Heavy bones. Leg bones. The claw bones. The teeth bones. The eye bones and tail bones, and the big old pieces of that. And that's how you make T Rex." Over time, teachers watch for storytelling and nonfiction registers to develop, and with that (as we discussed in the previous section), a sense of the overall structure of the piece.

Holistic Remembering

MISS ANN: This morning, Byron read *Silly Sally* (Wood 1992) word for word.
MISS KATE: He's memorized it. We've read it enough times!
MISS ANN: I don't know. It's different than memorizing. He really spends time with the pictures . . . stops to think . . . and sometimes even backs up to correct himself.

When children know books well, they often provide a holistic remembering as they read through a text, making it sound as if they have memorized it word for word. However, holistic remembering is a significant phase of reading development that goes beyond simple memorization. Rather than memorization, or only thinking about the words on a surface level, the child's focus in holistic remembering is on the reconstruction of meaning. Even children who have begun to make use of the graphophonic system will complete sentences with predictions that make sense rather than taking the time to go slowly or to sound out words. Holistic remembering provides evidence that children are developing awareness of the integrated quality of a text—of its cohesiveness and its connectedness from beginning to middle to end.

As with other aspects of language, the more familiar the child is with a book or story, the more confident and appropriate the child's response will be. The child's facility with oral storytelling may also play a role. Children who regularly engage in narrative-style interactions ("Chamika and I builded a snow fort . . . " "Our bus got in an accident . . . ") develop language knowledge that supports their construction of meaning from books (Schickedanz 1999). For example, as we mentioned earlier, the oral storytelling that occurs in many families helps children develop culturally appropriate ways to respond to narratives. Personal background and experience are always significant elements. Kidwatchers build on and respect such rich family experiences.

It is important to recognize that many children become tentative in their displays of literacy when they begin to know what they do not know. In terms of reading aloud, children are often willing to act as readers in response to pictures at a younger age but become hesitant to do so as they get older. In this case, "the child's unwillingness may indicate an increase in the child's understanding about the exactness and stability of stories when they are printed in books" (Schickedanz 1999, 85). Any time things seem to fall apart for children (when they seem to be more tentative in their responses), kidwatchers understand that what they are seeing may actually be a sign of progress.

Print to Meaning

Between the ages of four and six, most children begin to use the print itself to guide their reading. At this point, they understand that print plays a role in the reading of a book— we don't just make up what it says as we look at the illustrations or rely on our memories to tell the story. Children often begin to read without being fully aware of word boundaries, punctuation, or the concepts represented by the terms *letter*, *word*, and *sound*. For example, if given the opportunity, some children read while adults finger point, predicting words or phrases appropriately and using some graphophonic cues. Others read along with print until they hear the sentence is almost over, and then supply the rest through prediction or memory. Others point to each word as it is being read, chiming in when they can. Others scan the print, focusing in to remember certain names, words, or phrases. Observing children's holistic remembering reveals that, although they are not fully able to use print continuously, at certain moments, print takes on significance, and is used to construct meaning. Documenting children's knowledge as they read and reread familiar text helps teachers to track their growth and to understand how they are learning to comprehend— to make meaning from print.

Interaction and Observation

We have emphasized the importance of children becoming familiar with (1) the functions of books; (2) routines for sharing books; (3) discourses for talking about books; and (4) concepts and strategies for comprehending or constructing a meaningful text. In a kidwatching classroom, teachers interact with children with the intention of helping them develop in each of these areas. As appropriate, they use anecdotal notes and/or checklists (described later in this chapter) to help them reflect on what children know and to document their knowledge and growth.

Another important part of a teacher's book-handling interactions involves asking questions to reveal how and what children are thinking. Figure 4–1 provides an example set of questions that may be helpful in understanding children's concepts, attitudes, and perceptions about reading.

When supporting and observing children's development of book-handling knowledge, keep in mind that children develop concepts about print not only from handling and sharing books but also from countless other daily experiences with the print in their homes and communities. When interacting with children around books, therefore, it is a good idea to trust that they already have myriad knowledge that supports their meaning making. Along with your teaching interactions, allow time for independent and child-

led explorations so that children may refine and develop their own hypotheses, and so that you have opportunities to observe and document their knowledge. Anecdotal notes, checklists, and the more formal Book-Handling Knowledge Task (see Figure 4–4) can be used to structure your observations.

Anecdotal Notes

One observational tool for documenting book-handling knowledge is anecdotal notes. The following questions may be selected to guide your observations, and different answers may be documented at different times:

▶ What kinds of books appeal to the child? What books does the child choose to read?

▶ What functions do books serve for the child at home; at school?

▶ With whom does the child seem comfortable reading? What is the nature of the child's transactions with books when reading with this person?

▶ What is the nature of the child's transactions when reading and listening to books in whole-class settings; small groups; one-to-one?

▶ What book-sharing routines seem comfortable to the child?

▶ Does the child usually discuss/transact with books in the first or second language?

▶ How would I describe the child's self-concept as a reader?

▶ What book-handling knowledge and print concepts does the child demonstrate? What are the child's concepts of directionality? Has the child discovered that print does the telling? What are the child's concepts of words and letters? What connections is the child beginning to make between print and meaning?

▶ What knowledge do the child's miscues and inventions reveal (see Chapter 6)?

Name: _____ Date_____ Age_____

1. Do you know how to read?

   If yes:

   a. How did you learn how to read?

   b. Did somebody help you to learn or did you learn by yourself? (If yes, who?)

   c. Do you like to read?

   d. What do you like to read?

   If no:

   a. Do you want to be able to read?

   b. How will you learn to read?

   c. Does someone have to help you learn how to read?

   d. Who do you think will help you learn how to read?

2. Is it possible to learn to read by yourself?

3. Is learning to read easy or hard?

4. Why do you think learning to read is easy/hard?

5. Do the people you live with know how to read?

   a. What do they read?

   b. Where do they read? (kitchen, living room)

   c. What language do they read?

6. Do the people you live with ever read to you?

   a. Who?

   b. What do they read?

   c. In what language do they read to you?

   d. Do you like it? Why?

7. What do you look at while you are being read to? Anything else?

8. a. If I said, "I'm going to read you a story," what would I do?

   b. If I said, "I'm going to tell you a story," what would I do?

   c. Are reading a story and telling a story the same or different? How?

9. Can you read with your eyes closed? How?

10. Do you have a TV? Is there anything to read on TV? Do you have a computer? What is there to read on a computer?

11. Do you ever go to the store?

    a. Is there anything in the store that you read or people can read?

    b. What? (Try to get at books, magazines, newspapers, signs, and labels without using those words. If not, ask directly about them.)

12. Why do people read?

Adapted from Y. Goodman (1992)

Reproducible, see p. 103

FIGURE 4–1   Child's Concepts of Reading

► What kinds of information does the child include when reading text aloud? Does the child show control over the beginning, middle, and ending of a story? Does the child use a storytelling discourse? What kind of language does the child use when reading different forms of nonfiction?

► How are the child's book-handling concepts changing over time?

Checklists

Children's book-handling knowledge is also documented through checklists or observational forms, which are kept in a child's work folder and/or cumulative folder for over-time comparisons. As children have choice time, work with you in small groups, read in teams, or read independently, observational checklists and forms are useful in assessing a wide range of strategies. Figures 4–2 and 4–3 provide examples of such checklists/forms. Family members and visiting adults often participate in these evaluations.

Book-Handling Knowledge

A more formal book-handling interaction enables you to determine what children know about reading specific literacy materials, and to determine areas needing further support.

Child's Name: _____

Instructions: Use the blank spaces to fill in the dates on which the following concepts are observed.

Handling

_____ Holds book in an upright position.
_____ Understands that print proceeds from left to right and top to bottom.
_____ Turns pages left to right.
_____ Reads print on left page before right page.
_____ Appropriately uses terms such as *cover, page, story, title,* and *author.* Others:
_____ _____ .
_____ Uses book title and cover illustration to make predictions.
_____ Understands that a book contains an author's message.
_____ Understands that an illustrator creates the visuals for a book.
_____ _____
_____ _____

Print Knowledge

_____ Understands that pictures are viewed and print is read.
_____ Knows what a *letter* is (names or points to a letter when asked; uses the term conventionally during conversations).
_____ Knows what a *word* is (names or points to a word when asked; uses the term conventionally during conversations).
_____ Participates in reading when the language is predictable.
_____ Attempts to match voice with print.
_____ Reads some words conventionally.
_____ _____
_____ _____

Interpretive Knowledge

_____ Is eager to select a book to read alone or to someone else.
_____ Is aware that books contain stories as well as other kinds of information.
_____ Labels pictures while looking through the pages of a book.
_____ Uses pictures to make up a connected story or sequence of events.
_____ Discusses/retells stories, referring to ___ character, ___setting, ___ problem, ___ plot episodes, ___ resolution, ___ theme.
_____ Discusses/retells key concepts and information learned from nonfiction.
_____ Retelling occurs in a logical sequence.
_____ Makes personal connections with books.
_____ Makes connections between books.
_____ _____
_____ _____

Reproducible, see p. 104

FIGURE 4–2   Informal Observation of Book Knowledge

Child's Name: _____ Date:_____

Choose a simple storybook. Title: _____

I would like you to read this book for me. Have you seen or read it before? _____

<u>If child says NO:</u>   <u>If child says YES:</u>
What do you think this book is about?   *What was the book about?*
_____ Uses illustrations   _____ Brief response
_____ Uses illustrations and makes   _____ Detailed response
      additional inferences   _____ Uses print
_____ Uses print

Show me the front of the book. Show me the back. Where is the title?
_____ Front   _____ Back   _____ Title

*Open the book to where the story begins. Response:*_____

Show me where you read. Use your finger to show me how you read.
_____ Points to pictures   _____ Points to words
_____ Goes left to right   _____ Uses return sweep

Read the book. (If the child refuses, prompt with Pretend to read or Use the pictures.)
_____ No response
_____ Uses picture cues to label
_____ Uses picture cues to construct a meaningful, connected story
_____ Reads some of the words in the book
_____ Reads the words

After reading, the child:
_____ Can point to a capital letter; _____ lowercase letter.
_____ Can frame one word; _____ two words; _____ first word; _____ last word.
_____ Can frame one letter; _____ two letters; _____ first letter; _____ last letter.
_____ Can frame a period; _____ a comma; _____ a question mark; _____ quotation marks.
_____ Can track 4–5 lines of print as you read them.
_____ Can read some words. List:_____

Tell me something about the story: _____
_____
_____
_____

Did you like this book? _____ *Why?* _____
_____
_____
_____

Reproducible, see p. 105

FIGURE 4–3   Book-Handling and Print Concepts

Name: _____ Date_____ Age_____

Item	Administration	Instruction	Possible Responses	Child's Response
1	Show book; title covered by hand.	"What's this?" If child answers with name of book, record and ask, "What's (name of book given by child, e.g., *The Hungry Caterpillar*)?"	"book" "storybook" "story" name of book	
2	Display book.	"What do you do with it?"	"read it" "look at it" "tell it" "open it"	
3		"What's inside it?"	"story" "picture" "words" "pages" "letters" "things"	
4	Hold on to a page.	"Show me a page in this book." / "Is this a page?"	Points to page. / "yes"	
5		"Show me the top of this page." / "Show me the bottom of this page."	Indicates top edge or toward top. / Indicates bottom of page or toward bottom.	
6	Present book upside down and back toward child.	"Show me the front of this book." / "Take the book and open it so that we can read it."	Any indication of front or first page. / Opens to first page.	
7		"Show me the beginning of the story." / "Show me the end of the story."	Points to first line or word of story. / Turns to last page and points to last line or word.	

Reproducible, see p. 106

Item	Administration	Instruction	Possible Responses	Child's Response
8	Turn back to beginning of story.	"Show me with your finger exactly where we have to begin reading."	Points to first word on page.	
9		"Show me with your finger which way we go as we read this page."	Left to right, on the page, with return sweep.	
10		"Where then?" (This may already have been done or stated in #8 or #9; if so, check off, but do not repeat.)	Top line to bottom line, with return sweep.	
11		"Read the book to me." If child declines, say, "Pretend to read it."	Record all responses.	
12	If child doesn't read book, or after child reads, continue.	"Now I'm going to read you this story. Show me where to start reading. Where do I begin?"	Indicates print on first page.	
13	Read one page.	"You point to the story while I read it." (Read slowly.)	Almost always matches spoken with written words. / Sometimes matches spoken with written words.	
14	If there is print on both pages, display the pages. / Read to end of story.	"Where do I go now?"	Points to the first line of print on the next page.	
15	If possible, turn to a page with print and a picture on it. Turn book upside down.	"Can you or I read this now?" "Why or why not?"	"Upside down."	

Reproducible, see p. 107

FIGURE 4–4   Book-Handling Knowledge

The task, created by Yetta (Goodman, Altwerger, and Marek 1989), is an adaptation of work by Marie Clay (1972) and David Doake (1988). The information collected during this interactional task is similar to that collected using Figure 4–3, but is more open-ended, provides more details, and relies on anecdotal notes. To implement the assessment, choose a picture storybook that the child is likely to find appealing or invite the child to select something he or she would enjoy looking at together with you. Sit side by side with the child so that both of you can easily see the print and pictures. Follow the procedures from Figure 4–4 (columns 1 and 2). Use columns 3 and 4 to record the child's responses. In the event that an expected response is given, items in column 3 are circled; column 4 is there to record any additional or unexpected responses. Some teachers audiotape these experiences to be able to verify responses and/or for comparison over time.

Connecting the Known with the New

As you come to understand your students' book-handling knowledge, it is important to

Item	Administration	Instruction	Possible Responses	Child's Response
16	Show student how to use masking cards to close "curtains" over "window." (Use two pieces of dark cardboard.)	"Let's put some of the story in this window. I want you to close the curtains like this until I can see just one letter." "Now just two letters."	One letter correct. Two letters correct.	
17	Open "curtains."	"Now close it until we can see just one word." "Now just two words."	One word correct. Two words correct.	
18	Open "curtains."	"Show me the first letter in a word, any word." "Show me the last letter in a word."	First correct. Last correct.	
19	Remove cards.	"Show me a capital letter, any capital letter."	Points clearly to a capital letter. Points to any letter.	
20	Close book and pass it to child.	"Show me the name of the book (or story)."	Cover, flyleaf, or title page.	
21	Get at comprehension.	"Tell me something about the story."	Record response.	
22	Title page pointing.	"It says here (read title) 'by (read author).' What does 'by (author's name, e.g., Angela Johnson)' mean?"	Responds appropriately.	
23	Title page pointing.	"It says here that the book is illustrated by (read illustrator). What does that mean?"	Responds appropriately.	

Reproducible, see p. 108

Reproducible, see p. 108

FIGURE 4–4   Continued

consider how they transfer this knowledge to other kinds of literacy materials. Knowing how to handle a storybook does not equate with knowing how to handle a nonfiction book, encyclopedia, or magazine. Lots of experience with particular types of text is necessary before children become skilled at using them. Therefore, we suggest adapting the book-handling task to support your observations of children handling varied kinds of text. Depending on your children and the literacy materials that are appropriate to their inquiries, the supplemental questions provided in Figure 4–5 may be relevant.

1. What's this called? (magazine, encyclopedia, newspaper)
2. What's inside?
3. Why do people read it?
4. Why did the author write it?
5. Show me what you do when you read a (name material).
6. How do you decide where to read?
7. Read to me.
8. What do you do when you don't want to read all of this, but want to find out about something in particular?
9. How do you use the pictures, diagrams, charts, maps, and so on?

FIGURE 4–5   Supplemental Questions for Extending Book-Handling Knowledge

Conclusion: Expanding Repertoires

By the time they come to school, many young children have a great deal of knowledge about books and book handling. Traditionally, schools have ignored this, planning literacy instruction as though children's knowledge were irrelevant, or as though the most important skills for reading were to learn letters and sounds. Careful documentation and analysis of children's book handling reveals that even very young readers are knowledgeable and use many strategies to construct meaning. Teachers document children's knowledge and strategies to develop a chronological record of their growth and to reveal the kinds of instruction they are likely to find comprehensible and relevant. They create a classroom environment in which children find reasons to read an ever richer range of genres for an ever widening range of purposes. With a thorough record of what children know about book handling, teachers are able to provide experiences and instruction that continue to build on children's strengths and give specialized attention to their needs.

Talk

"Mona, do you want to stir the bubbles?" Mona stirs as her grandmother reads aloud a bubble recipe, adding one ingredient at a time. "We're cooking bubbles," Mona says with satisfaction. Later, using a wand to blow and catch bubbles, she shouts, "I catched-ed one! I catched-ed a bubble!" Her older sister responds: "You caught one? How did you do that?"

Children are language learners by virtue of being born into human society. They construct knowledge about language as they use it to engage with the people and objects in their environments and to make sense of their sur-

roundings (Halliday 1975). Mona's example, and others in this chapter, illustrates that expansion of oral language and extension of learning happen simultaneously within the highly contextualized settings of early childhood worlds. It is under the influence of their own daily talk and actions, as well as the responses of their family and community, that children expand and fine-tune both their linguistic and their conceptual knowledge. Most language development scholars and researchers agree that children control most features of the grammar of their mother tongue by the time they come to kindergarten.

Why Talk?

Kidwatchers are interested in children's oral language for two major reasons. First, they know that it is the primary symbol system through which children learn about the world. As we will see, children use talk to facilitate their own thinking and learning in all subject areas, and to jointly construct meaning and knowledge with others. Second, kidwatchers value children's talk because it is a window into their knowledge and thinking. Observing and documenting children's talk reveals their knowledge of language functions and forms, their interactional competencies, and what they know about the world around them. The more teachers listen to children talk, the more they see how talk works hand in hand with reading and writing to develop all aspects of language and thinking. As you document, keep in mind that talk in the classroom also involves listening. When we consider talk, we also consider the listening capabilities of children as they attend to their peers and the adults in the community. In this chapter we first explore the ways in which talk facilitates development. Then, we describe the ways in which kidwatchers document and evaluate children's talk and listening, and use what they learn to sensitively support their development.

A Medium for Thinking and Learning

Harry (age five) and Karla (age four) are writing and drawing together. Harry writes "M-O-M."

HARRY: That spells *mom*, I think.
KARLA: If that's the way you *think* you spell *mom*, then *spell mom*.
HARRY: You know what? I think that's really how you spell *mom*. You know why? Because at kindergarten today we had to spell *mom*, and I think I remember how to spell *mom*. M-O-M. [*then, pointing to each letter as if to confirm what he is saying*] Mah . . . oh . . . mom.

Oral language is a medium through which children expand their concepts of the world, including their literacy concepts. Through language, children come face-to-face with their own ideas and, therefore, open them up to new levels of consideration. "Language enables the child to make his idea into a *thing*, an object, an entity that he can refine, consider, shape, and act on . . . " (Lindfors 1991, 9). For example, Harry has been taught to spell *mom* at kindergarten but uses oral language to reconstruct for himself how it is spelled and why it is spelled that way. By bringing his ideas to a talking place, he is able to shape and reflect on them and, therefore, to shape and expand his thinking.

According to Vygotsky (1978), oral language plays a central role in children's internalization of all cultural knowledge and mental processes. Children learn as a result of interacting socially and transforming the language and actions of their social experiences into tools for independent thinking. Transformation is not akin to copying, mimicking, or imitating but instead involves a process of *internalization*, in which children select, reconstruct, and modify the communicative and problem-solving tools of their society to meet their own needs. To be a successful language user, Harry must modify and reconstruct the information he experiences socially (including information about spelling) to make it understandable and workable for him. His "mah . . . oh . . . mom" (like Mona's "catched-ed" overgeneralization) is evidence that children are active sense makers, inventing their own ways of saying things as they are figuring out how language works.

Vygotsky believes that private speech (speech not directed at others, but often taking place in the presence of others) is a transitional medium for internalizing social experiences—a tool that helps children gradually develop control over complex concepts. Initially, "children solve practical tasks with the help of their speech, as well as their eyes and hands" (Vygotsky 1978, 26): as they spell, they make sounds aloud; as they compose, they provide oral narratives; as they listen to stories, they say what they are thinking; as they encounter difficult text, they read aloud. "Sometimes speech becomes of such vital importance that, if not permitted to use it, young children cannot accomplish the given task" (26). Private speech is a tool for internalizing socially learned processes and transforming them into tools for independent thinking.

While all of children's talk is of interest to kidwatchers, their questions and wonderings are particularly significant. Questions and wonderings are an ideal point at which new learning can take place. Consider the situation in which four-year-old Miguel asks, "How come cheese is not sticky, but it sticks to this [tortilla]?" At such a point, the child has searched for and initiated what he wants to know, and placed himself in a position to use talk to revise his growing theory of the world (Lindfors 1991). An adult who takes initiative at the point of a question or wondering is likely to find a child in his or her zone of proximal development—the place where personal curiosity is aroused and meaningful learning can take place. But, let us rush to say that input from another person is not always needed in order for learning to occur. As important as the social environment is, sometimes when children question and wonder, just the act of thinking—personal inquiry—results in changing conceptions (Oakes and Lipton 1999). We do not teach children all that they know. As active thinkers and language users, they are always learning by sorting out the tensions between social conventions and their own inventions; always trying to make sense of the world and making many discoveries and connections through their own mental processes.

A Medium for Jointly Constructing Knowledge

ANGIE: I just wrote B-E-A-I-G-I-E-W-E.

KARLA: I know what you wrote. This is your name—this . . . *Is* this your name?

ANGIE: No.

KARLA: What is—um, it *is* your name, but it's not—but you're not—pretending—it's not—

ANGIE: No, it's *not* my name! I know. It's A-N-G-I-E.

KARLA: Oh yeah. But some of those are in your name, right?

ANGIE: Yeah, like A, G, I, G, E, right?

KARLA: Yeah, and then this E [*pointing*].

So far, we have placed our focus on the role of language in supporting individual children's processes of constructing knowledge. Another important matter to consider is the role that language plays in supporting children in jointly, or collaboratively, constructing knowledge. Classroom literacy events are often characterized by children formulating and testing ideas and hypotheses socially—a process that is highly facilitative of their development. For example, talking with Angie gives Karla the opportunity to sort out the notion that there is a difference between unordered (random) letters being used to spell a word and letters that are purposefully ordered. To this point, Karla has not yet incorporated this understanding into her writing. Angie benefits from the exchange, too. As she listens to clarify what Karla knows, she gains experience with taking the perspective of another person. The talk in this event is a tool for these children to bring their implicit understandings and personal knowledge to a meeting place where they can construct new understandings together.

Each classroom literacy event is an opportunity for children to construct knowledge together—to articulate and share information about their hypotheses and ideas, to see how others respond to them, and to see how others approach literacy-related tasks. Children's ordinary conversations and talking-through procedures teach them to recount and reinterpret events, to display their abilities, to share the process of how they do things, and to encounter and understand the logic behind different points of view—processes that are essential for ultimate success in reading and writing (Graves 1989). Harry's, Angie's, and Karla's talk experiences illustrate that "children benefit from learning situations that allow them to explore and to experience in their own ways the symbolic and social medium they are learning" (Dyson 1989, 271).

Interactions with Children

Kidwatchers take quite seriously their role in facilitating children's talk. Skillful kidwatchers learn to listen to children's language and to use it as a platform for supporting their thinking. Kidlistening is integral to kidwatching. Rather than focusing on language instruction separately from social interactions, kidwatchers focus on helping children expand their uses of language as a tool for thought and action. The following sections describe some of the typical talk strategies teachers use to simultaneously support children's linguistic and conceptual growth, to ensure that one mutually builds on and nourishes the other.

Let Children Do the Talking

As Hannah is reading a short story to her teacher, she pauses to reflect on her thinking:

HANNAH: I can read the word *because*, but I can't remember how to spell it.
TEACHER: Yeah. Hmm. Why do you think that is?
HANNAH: Maybe because when I *look* at it—it's already there, and so, like, I just have to—all I have to do is remember what it looks like. But when I have to spell it, I have to think of all the letters, all by myself.

The best way to simultaneously support children's language and conceptual growth is to encourage their talk. As we have seen, talk is a valuable tool for thinking, learning, and jointly constructing knowledge. In the example, Hannah is the talker, with the teacher playing a supporting role. As such, it is the child's questions and thoughts that drive the interaction. Unafraid to let children take the lead in classroom learning, kidwatchers genuinely listen to their talk and thoughtfully respond to their ideas. Through listening and responding, they learn what children

know, what's hard for them, and what's easy, enabling themselves to sensitively build on children's conceptualizations.

If you reread Hannah's example and Karla's example in the previous section, you will notice that their talk is *exploratory*—characterized by a hesitant, fragmented verbal construction and reconstruction of ideas (Barnes 1993). Karla seems uncertain of what she wants to say and how to say it, and almost sounds as if she is thinking aloud. Hannah seems forced by her language to clarify for herself what she is thinking. "The struggle to communicate with someone who only half understands can contribute to the clarification of the speaker's own thinking . . . students' own efforts to express their understandings are a major means of enhancing learning" (Barnes 1993, 344). Often, when children struggle with language, teachers supply the tough expressions for them. Yet, "the struggle itself is important for both the child's thinking and for his languaging. If we can hold our tongues, we do the child a service. There is no surer way for him to become the master of idea than to render it expressible" (Lindfors 1991, 268).

Jointly Negotiate Concepts

At recess, Evan is playing with a small toy, but when his fingers become too cold, he brings it inside to his teacher, Christian Bush.

EVAN: [*opening and closing his hands*] My hands were too cold to play with it. Now, they're evaporating.
CHRISTIAN: [*taking one of his cold hands between her warm hands*] Let's see . . . what other word could describe what you are feeling—because, remember what *evaporation* means?
EVAN: [*looks up for a moment, as if thinking*] Oh yeah. [*thinks some more*] Vibrating. They're vibrating.
CHRISTIAN: Vibrating. Frostbit. Thawing.

Another way to support children's linguistic and conceptual development is to jointly negotiate concepts with them. Joint negotiation is characterized by meaningful activity in which the teacher and child work together toward a goal or solution, with the teacher using language that is just beyond what the child might use independently. Teachers "speak at the level where . . . children can comprehend them and [they] move ahead with remarkable sensitivity to [the] child's progress" (Bruner 1983, 39). Such communications help children learn how to extend their language into new contexts and settings. Joint negotiation makes sense because it occurs within children's zones of proximal development. Teachers follow and lead at the same time, listening to children and inspiring uses of language that are just beyond what they might use on their own.

Encourage Reflection

Christian is teaching her students how to write a script.

> CHRISTIAN: Now, tell us what a script is, Max—and I'm asking Max because he's already had experience with this.
>
> MAX: It's a piece of paper where you write down what you're going to do in the puppet show. Because, if you don't write it, you're going to mess up and you have to start over and over again.
>
> CHRISTIAN: Max, do you remember when you wrote down what each person was going to say? Why was that important?
>
> MAX: Because if you don't write it out, people won't know what to say and they will talk at the same time.

A third way of supporting children's linguistic and conceptual development is to encourage reflective dialogue. The goal is to raise issues and pose questions that help children to reflect on what they know, and to relate new concepts and ideas to those they have developed already. In teaching scriptwriting, for example, Christian does not simply tell her students what to do. Instead, letting Max take the lead, she helps them analyze the format of a script and think about why its particular form is important. Christian under-

stands that children learn not through doing only, but through reflecting on doing (Adelman 1992). If she wants them to internalize the concepts she is teaching, they need to reflect on why and how they work. To encourage reflection, Christian typically asks children questions about what they know, how they know, how they learned it, and why things work the way they do. Asking such questions not only prompts children to visit, revisit, reflect on, and share their thinking processes, it also shows them that these thinking processes are important.

Provide Substantive Responses

Which column contains the substantive responses?

Column A	Column B
I liked your demonstration.	What kind of practice did it take to get ready for this demonstration?
You listened well today.	You seemed very interested today. What caught your interest?
Your pictures are great.	Your pictures helped me enjoy your story. How did you think to include the little anchor?

Another way to simultaneously support children's linguistic and conceptual development is to provide substantive responses to their demonstrations of knowledge. Clearly, the responses given in column B are more substantive than those in column A. They point to a particular strength or competency, rather than being general in nature or focused on praising the child, and they prompt children to talk and think further. In addition to a specific focus on children's actions, the teacher's language focuses on their thinking. Kidwatchers attempt feedback that is primarily substantive because it keeps student language going and fosters its further development. Substantive responses show children that teachers are aware of their developing competencies, acquaint children with the descriptive terms

used by adults, help them reflect back on the work they have done, and, overall, serve to keep their language going.

A Rich Talk Environment

If we want children's language to come to life in the classroom, we have to provide a rich environment for learning. Christian is a first-grade teacher who has arranged to do just that. Enter her classroom at almost any time of day, and you are likely to notice that it is a lively place for inquiry, collaboration, thinking, teaching, sharing, laughing, and learning. The children's talk tells it all:

"Pee pi po pum. Who's that walking on my bridge? I'm going to eat you up."

"How do you spell *bite?*"
"B-I-T."
"How do you spell *are?*"

"That's the easiest word in the world! R!"

"Cheetahs can run 70 miles an hour. *Miles.* M-I-L-S."
   "No, Max, it's M-I-L-Z."
   "Z? Don't just think that Z makes the same kind of S."

"Once when I was little I had to stay in a hospital and I had the 'monia. And I was like three months—five months old and they had to put me in a crib and . . . "

Observing Christian's students at work and play, it is easy to see that they are simultaneously making discoveries about language and the world. In such an environment, knowledge about one feeds knowledge about the other, and mutually, they spiral toward higher planes.

What is Christian's role in arranging such an environment? First, in collaboration with her students, she enacts a curriculum that inspires their *interests*. Using district and state materials as general guidelines, she lets children's questions, wonderings, and knowledge determine the specifics of what they will do. If Christian were to do all the deciding, the curriculum would belong to her, and the children would need to do little talking, thinking, and learning. As it stands, they want to share their knowledge and use language to question, inquire, and think.

Second, Christian ensures that her students find a variety of *reasons to use language* to explore curricular concepts. Depending on the conceptual goal (let's say it's to compare their community and region with others), she may encourage them to tell stories, retell events, report information, request information, explain how to do something, plan an event, or pose a problem. As the functional need to use language arises, Christian teaches elements of form. On myriad occasions, she demonstrates the language that learners use to organize and inquire about the world. For example, when the children expressed an interest in performing puppet shows, she taught them how scripts are organized. When groups needed a way to efficiently share what they were learning, she showed them how to use a chart to organize information. When they wanted to tell others about stories they had read, she demonstrated the use of story webs. When they were collecting information about families, she taught them how to conduct an interview. The quality and range of opportunities children have to use oral language significantly affect their progress and development as talkers, listeners, and learners (Barr et al. 1999).

Third, the physical environment in Christian's classroom *promotes socialization*. The furniture is arranged to support whole-group meetings (a large rug with a stool), small-group work (a class library, work centers, tables, beanbag chairs, pillows, and empty floor space), and pairs working together (plenty of inviting nooks and crannies, and a computer with two chairs). Depending on the children's

needs, they quickly find appropriate spaces in which to work together.

Fourth, Christian believes that a sense of *safe community* is essential if learning is to occur to its fullest potential. In order for the social environment to promote talk, children must find themselves in a community that is welcoming of many language possibilities. Children, regardless of language or dialects spoken, regardless of conceptual understandings, and regardless of facility with language, are encouraged to take the risks associated with using talk to try out new ideas and to build knowledge together. Christian helps her students feel safe by fostering a classroom culture in which all children are seen as competent to read, write, and talk. From day one, she responds to children claiming they "can't" with, "Well, show me what you *can* do, so I can help you grow," or "Could you *pretend* to [write or read]? That will give us a place to begin." Children who are hesitant to talk are helped to develop strategies for group participation: "Tell us what you drew." "If you can't read what you wrote, then *tell* us about it." When a child says something that is treated as "out of whack" by other children, Christian responds with, "Wait. Everyone sees things differently. Let's listen so we can see in a new way." Throughout the year, she makes a point to help students understand that language and literacy develop over time; children do not write or draw or talk like adults, nor does she expect them to do so. Christian's focus is on developing a classroom culture in which learners take risks with language and actively, sensitively listen to what others have to say.

Finally, with Christian's help, her students have learned that there are twenty-nine *experts* in the classroom, each with unique and important knowledge. Children as well as adults have funds of knowledge that enrich the classroom community. For example, Evan and Cayla know how to spell lots of hard words and can read almost any print in the classroom; Max and Mark know how to organize a script and put together a puppet show; Kiara knows how to fix the classroom pencil sharpener, and is even good at unclogging the tiny ones brought from home; Jake knows lots about insects, and for that matter, knows lots about just about everything. In a classroom full of experts, where children have a say in what they learn and how they learn, language and concepts are inextricably linked and grow in new directions together.

Guidelines for Observation and Documentation

There is no question that talk has a tremendous impact on what and how children learn. If we want to develop appropriate educational experiences for children, we must listen to them talk. Observations of children's talk in a variety of settings help teachers develop insight into their language and conceptual growth and evaluate the ways in which the talk environment promotes or detracts from learning. Teachers document talk primarily through anecdotal records, field notes, and audiotapes. Depending on the teacher's purpose, brief quotes are documented on sticky notes or clipboards (accessible around the room) and longer stretches of talk are recorded and then transcribed or listened to at a later time. The following sections comprise a framework to consider when evaluating talk and the talk environment. The items for evaluation focus on observing children (1) as they talk and listen in different situations and settings; (2) as they explore different language functions and forms; (3) as they demonstrate different interactional competencies; and (4) as they demonstrate language and conceptual knowledge about various aspects of the world. The items should not be viewed as absolutes but should be altered and carefully selected to suit your evaluation purposes.

Observing Talk in Different Contexts

Kidwatchers observe children as they talk and listen in different situations and settings to identify the learning contexts in which they seem most comfortable, and those in which they need most support. Figure 5–1 lists some important groupings and kinds of talk/

_____ Whole Class	_____ Individual Child: _____
Self-Talk	
One-to-One with Adult	
One-to-One with Peers (record peer names)	
Self-Chosen Peer Group (list names)	
Teacher-Chosen Peer Group (needs-based; children who seldom talk in groups; children who talk often; etc.)	
Small Instructional Group (observe across changes in subject matter)	
Whole Group	
Play Settings	

Reproducible, see p. 109

FIGURE 5–1   Talk Contexts

listening to consider. You may use this as an anecdotal note-taking form on a case-by-case basis with any child who seems to be struggling in the talk environment, or as a tool for evaluating the overall quality of talk in your classroom. Either way, make a plan to observe four or five instances of each category on the form, and then develop a set of questions or use questions such as those listed in the first two sections of Figure 5–2 to focus your analysis.

Observing Language Functions and Forms

Another important lens for evaluating talk is in terms of the functions it serves in facilitating communication and learning. _Functions_ refer to the reasons or purposes for using language, such as to report information or express

Questions for Documenting and Supporting Individual Children's Growth
- How comfortable is the child speaking with the teacher, one other child, small groups? How does this change across contexts and subject matter?
- How is the child using talk as a tool for learning and thinking? How does this change across contexts?
- In what situations and settings does the child benefit most from language use?
- If the child speaks two languages, how does language use vary across contexts and subject matter?

Questions for Evaluating the Talk Environment
- Which settings, situations, and experiences promote exploratory talk and which do not?
- Who is doing most of the talk in various settings? How does this affect the quality of learning for all children?
- Whose talk is valued/whose questions do we pursue as a class? What is the nature of these questions?
- What evidence do I have that children who do not talk much are learning, listening intently, expanding their functional uses of language, and developing their interactional competencies?
- In any given setting, how does talk relate to what children are reading and writing, and to other classroom learning experiences (Wells 1990)?
- What questions do children ask? What do their questions indicate about their views of what is important? Who do they ask?

Questions for Teacher Self-Evaluation
- How do I jointly negotiate concepts with students? How do I encourage them to use language to reflect on their ideas and thinking? What is the nature of my questioning? What is the nature of my feedback?
- What functions and interactional competencies do I value? What topics do I value? Is the classroom environment conducive to exploring a variety of functions and topics?
- How do I support children in expanding their functions and interactional competencies?
- How would I characterize my own talk in various situations and settings?
- Have I learned to value new kinds of talk? Have I learned to value quiet listeners?
- How do I support *all* of my students in using language to learn, including bilingual students?

FIGURE 5–2   Questions for Evaluating Talk

a point of view. The goals in evaluating children's functional uses of language are to ensure that (1) classroom talk serves as a tool for children to construct and express knowledge in a variety of ways, and (2) children's language learning constantly reaches out to meet new challenges. Figure 5–3 lists some specific language functions that foster classroom learning. One way to use Figure 5–3 is as a quick check to ensure that your classroom provides opportunities for children to construct and express knowledge in a variety of ways. We suggest that you use the list to make your own chart of the functions that are most important in your classroom. Another way to use Figure

5–3 is as a tool to document the knowledge and growth of each child, or of particular children who may need extra support in the areas listed.

With every function comes a set of language forms, or structures that take their shape depending on the purpose and meaning of the language. For example, "Let's pretend" and "Once upon a time" are forms conducive to creating imaginative worlds. "First . . . next . . . last . . . " and "Here's how I do it . . . " are forms conducive to explaining how to do or make something. If children are exploring a variety of functions, rest assured that they are exploring a variety of forms. Just "create the

Place a check by the functions that are regularly present in your classroom. Place a star by those that occur in various contexts and settings. Indicate the extent to which languages other than English are used to serve the varying functions.

_____ Sharing stories

_____ Retelling events

_____ Reporting information

_____ Explaining how to do or make something

_____ Expressing language and literacy knowledge

_____ Building productive learning relationships with peers and adults

_____ Creating imaginative worlds (during play; through writing or drawing; while singing)

_____ Taking social action

_____ Planning events

_____ Enjoying language for its aesthetic value (poetry; language play)

_____ Describing sensory experiences (sights, smells, sounds, touches, tastes)

_____ Expressing feelings, empathy, emotional identification

_____ Expressing points of view

_____ Taking leadership

_____ Asking questions; requesting information

_____ Building collaborative relations

_____ Responding to peers' and teachers' questions and requests for information

_____ _____

_____ _____

Reproducible, see p. 110

FIGURE 5–3   Oral Language Functions: Classroom Observation

Child's Name: _____ Date _____ Age _____

Shares stories

Retells events

Explains how to do or make something

Creates imaginative worlds (during play; through writing or drawing; while singing)

Plans events

Enjoys language for its aesthetic value (poetry; language play)

Expresses feelings, empathy, emotional identification

Takes leadership

Reproducible, see p. 111

FIGURE 5–4   Oral Language Functions: Individual Observation

context and the rest will follow" (Short, Harste, and Burke 1996, 10).

When examining the functions listed in Figure 5–3, it is important to recognize that oral facility with each of these supports written facility. For example, children who learn to report information or explain how to do something have important knowledge for writing nonfiction text. Children who can tell a cohesive, logically sequenced story have important understandings for structuring a story in writing. Children who learn to freshly describe a feeling or sensory experience become successful poetry writers. At times, teachers act as scribes, to demonstrate how oral language changes as it is transformed to written forms.

Over time, teachers watch for children to expand and fine-tune their uses of language functions and forms. Figure 5–4 shows an adapted version of Figure 5–3, developed for observing individuals. Even if you just check off the items for individual children, or take brief notes, parents find conversations around such forms useful in understanding the kinds of language that are supportive of school learning. Also, parents may offer insights into children's thinking and language uses that have not been visible to you in the school setting.

Observing Interactional Competencies
Along with monitoring children's exploration of language functions and forms, kidwatchers

monitor their interactional competencies. Figure 5–5 lists a set of competencies that support children's learning and interacting in a classroom setting. Because each child and each group is unique, it is a good idea to adapt the list to meet the needs of your particular students. As you develop your own form, you may wish to leave space to record anecdotes and examples. This will be particularly helpful if you plan to use it on a case-by-case basis with children who are struggling in the talk environment, or if you plan to share detailed information with parents.

In general, over the course of the year, kidwatchers document children's interactional competencies to ensure that they are developing their capabilities to use language to learn, and that they are demonstrating empathy and careful attention to the feelings and views of others. They collaborate and conference often with children and parents as they document and reflect. Not only does this bring to light (for all of you) the competencies that are conducive to classroom learning, it also helps you in understanding the competencies children may be demonstrating at home but not in school. Locating instances of success outside of school helps you bring such instances into the classroom.

Observing Knowledge Demonstrated Through Talk

We have discussed ways of observing children's functional uses of language, as well as their interactional competencies. We also believe it is important to observe and document the general knowledge children demonstrate through talk. As we have said all along, kidwatchers regularly ask:

1. What does the child know about language?
2. What evidence is there that development is taking place?
3. When a child produces unexpected or unconventional language, what does it tell about the child's knowledge?

These questions may be extended into content areas. For example, as part of a class inquiry focused on insects, you might ask:

1. What scientific language does the child use to construct and express knowledge about insects?
2. What evidence is there that the child is demonstrating more sophisticated uses of language in the talk about insects?
3. When the child uses language about insects unconventionally, what does it tell about the child's knowledge?

Learning any content involves learning the language needed to construct and express knowledge about that content. Talk is an ideal medium for monitoring children's con-

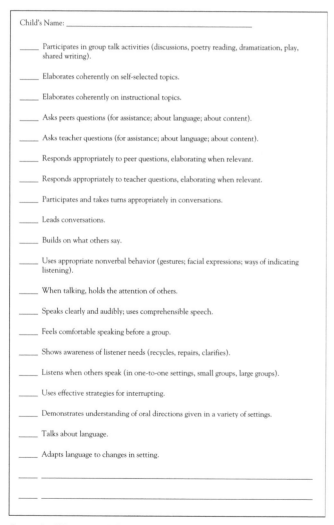

Child's Name: _____

_____ Participates in group talk activities (discussions, poetry reading, dramatization, play, shared writing).

_____ Elaborates coherently on self-selected topics.

_____ Elaborates coherently on instructional topics.

_____ Asks peers questions (for assistance; about language; about content).

_____ Asks teacher questions (for assistance; about language; about content).

_____ Responds appropriately to peer questions, elaborating when relevant.

_____ Responds appropriately to teacher questions, elaborating when relevant.

_____ Participates and takes turns appropriately in conversations.

_____ Leads conversations.

_____ Builds on what others say.

_____ Uses appropriate nonverbal behavior (gestures; facial expressions; ways of indicating listening).

_____ When talking, holds the attention of others.

_____ Speaks clearly and audibly; uses comprehensible speech.

_____ Feels comfortable speaking before a group.

_____ Shows awareness of listener needs (recycles, repairs, clarifies).

_____ Listens when others speak (in one-to-one settings, small groups, large groups).

_____ Uses effective strategies for interrupting.

_____ Demonstrates understanding of oral directions given in a variety of settings.

_____ Talks about language.

_____ Adapts language to changes in setting.

_____ _____

_____ _____

Reproducible, see p. 112

FIGURE 5–5   Interactional Competencies

ceptual and linguistic growth in all content areas.

An Environment That Recognizes Difference

Part of your growth as a kidwatcher will involve making continual efforts to learn about language differences that may be a result of children's membership in varying language and cultural groups, and to clarify and analyze your understandings, attitudes, and perceptions about these differences. "As teachers of children from different cultural backgrounds, we need to understand that our particular language and literacy socialization in large part contributes to how we interpret and generate classroom activities. The more we learn about the diverse experiences and needs of our students, the better prepared we will be to question existing practices and create educationally and culturally appropriate activities for all of our students" (Faltis 1997, 27–28).

Kidwatchers make a conscious effort to deconstruct the implicit assumptions they may have developed, and to consider the role these assumptions play in creating conditions for learning. Following is a set of linguistic and cultural characteristics to consider as a starting point for reflection. Any of the items in the set may vary across individuals within your classroom community. Your task is to consider what these variations mean to you, and how they influence your interactions with children. Children demonstrate varying

► orientations toward public performance (feelings about speaking in front of a group; feelings about publicly demonstrating knowledge)

► patterns of turn taking (overlapping vs. clear-cut turns; ways of using pauses; perceptions of what constitutes an interruption; echoing)

► question/answer practices (levels of familiarity with being asked questions to

which the adult already knows the answer, e.g., "What color is this?")

► sensitivity to language variation (tendencies to switch from one language or dialect to another; views of "low-status" dialects; capacities for speaking languages other than English in the classroom)

► uses of gesture and eye contact to show attention, understanding, emotion, and interest

► views of adult and child roles (expectations in terms of how much talk the child does; how much talk the adult does; what the child has license to say)

► orientations toward competition and collaboration

► ways of giving and receiving help

► ways of telling and interpreting stories

► word choices for conveying meanings ("That's dangerous" vs. "Get off that rail")

If you are interested in further reading, our list draws from the work of Erickson (1986), Faltis (1997), Heath (1983), Lindfors (1991), McWhorter (2000), Phillips (1983), Ruiz (1991), Smitherman (1999), Taylor (1983), and Wolfram, Adger, and Christian (1998). Their work has helped us to understand the importance of teachers valuing language diversity as a resource (rather than seeing it as a problem) and working to make their classrooms a place for all children to use language to its fullest potential—for communicating, learning, and thinking.

Student Self-Evaluation

As with any aspect of knowledge, it is important that students learn to evaluate their own use of talk. As teachers work with children in this area, they discuss with them what they need to do to make their communication successful. Figure 5–6 provides a list of items to consider for student self-evaluation.

- When is it easiest for me to talk? What makes it easy?
- When is it easiest for me to listen? What makes it easy?
- When is it hard for me to talk/listen? What makes it hard? What can I do to change this?
- With whom do I like to talk?
- Who is a good talker in our classroom? What makes that person good? What makes me a good talker?
- Who is a good listener? What makes that person good? What makes me a good listener?
- What kinds of things do I like to talk about? How can I use this to support my learning?
- Why do people talk? Why is it important that we talk in our classroom?
- How does my talk and listening help my group/our class have good discussions? What do I say that isn't helpful?
- How am I doing with sharing what I know or am learning with my classmates? With my teacher? With my family?

FIGURE 5–6 Questions for Student Self-Evaluation

Conclusion: Using What You Learn

Before children enter school, most of their language is celebrated. Families, caregivers, neighbors, and peers are excited by young children's attempts to communicate and seldom correct their grammar or phonology, but do respond to misconceptions about the world: "That's a plane, not a birdie." Intuitively they know that communication, rather than correctness, is the purpose of using language. Sometimes, however, when children move into schools, certain aspects of language learning are frowned upon and actually discouraged. Some children are not permitted to talk until their "work" is done; some are corrected each time they use language unconventionally. In some classrooms, the teacher does most of the talking. Some children learn very early that it is better to use language as little as possible in certain settings, notably—and regrettably—in the classroom.

Kidwatchers value talk. They know that embedded in a talk-filled classroom are the social supports that are central to the livelihood of the learning environment. Participating in talk helps children focus their thinking, make their implicit understandings more precise, and internalize cultural knowledge. It helps children articulate and refine their hypotheses and ideas, share information, and get feedback on their current knowledge and ways of knowing. In a classroom in which children have agency to talk and collaborate, they not only develop language, they develop their ability to use it as a tool for learning about the world.

Oral Reading and Miscues

Yetta is listening to her seven-year-old grandson Aaron read aloud to his three-year-old brother, who is cuddled with him on the sofa. He is reading a book called *The New Baby Calf*, which he has never heard or seen before (Goodman, Bird, and Goodman 1991, 102). He reads the title, turns to the first page of the story, and begins reading. The following excerpts are selected from the thirty-one-page story.

Text p. 4

Buttercup the cow had
a new baby calf,
a fine baby calf,
a strong baby calf,

Aaron Reads:

Buttercup the cow had
a new born calf,
a fine born calf,
a st . . . stug . . . starn . . .
soft baby calf.

Text p. 6

Not strong like
his mother,
But strong for a calf,
for this baby calf was
so new.

Not sarn . . . sarg like
his mother,
But   for a calf
for this born calf was
so new.

Text p. 8

Buttercup licked him	Buttercup licked . . . liked . . . licked him
with her strong warm tongue.	with her soft . . . tongue.
Buttercup washed him	Buttercup was had . . . was had . . . washed him
with her strong warm tongue.	with her soft warrrr . . . um tongue.

Text p. 10

And the new baby calf liked that!	And the new baby calf liked that!

Aaron's reading reveals a great deal about himself as a developing reader of pictures and print, and about the reading process in general. He quickly examines the fine illustrations of farm life whenever he turns a page and then reads from the print on the left-hand page, starting at the top and returning to the beginning of the next line. He is capable of book handling, knowing where the story starts and how to follow the written text from left to right, top to bottom, and page to page. He knows that the pictures are helpful to his reading, but he uses them selectively, usually when he comes to an unfamiliar noun, verb, or adjective. He doesn't look at the pictures when he reads function words (such as *the*, *with*, *and*, or *very*) that he knows do not appear in pictures.

Aaron's intonation reveals that he is usually sensitive to literary language. However, at times, he reads slowly, hesitating when he is unfamiliar with some of the language or when the grammar does not make sense to him. He predicts when he reads *new born calf* for *new baby calf*. This results in acceptable sentences and he doesn't correct them because they sound like language and make sense in the story. Aaron may be more familiar with *baby* as a noun than an adjective, but by page 10, he learns that *baby* can be an adjective in certain contexts. Maybe this is because now that he has seen *baby* a number of times, he is aware that it has some letter patterns that do not represent the sounds in *born*. Once he knows *baby* in this context, he does

not miscue on it again. Aaron also predicts *soft tongue* for *strong tongue*. When sentences sound acceptable to him, he confirms his miscues and does not self-correct.

But he does self-correct in contexts where he knows he is reading unacceptable sentences. He predicts *licked* appropriately on page 8, but *liked* also fits the meaning and is confirmed by his graphophonic knowledge, so he reads *liked* and then self-corrects back to *licked* as he perceives *with her tongue*. This shows he is always monitoring his reading, confirming his predictions of the meaning of the story (semantics), the grammar of the sentences (syntax), and the systematic relations between the patterns of letters and the patterns of sounds in English (graphophonics). He also self-corrects his substitution of *was had* for *washed*, first carefully sounding out but then using his meaning-making strategies to self-correct. His substitutions and the words without miscues show his knowledge of the graphophonic system of English. He also sounds out unfamiliar words such as *strong*. Unsuccessful at first, he keeps working at it, substituting *soft* on page 4, omitting the word on page 6, and substituting *soft* again on page 8. However, on page 20 (not shown), when the baby calf takes a walk, the text says: *A little longer walk, A little stronger walk*. In this context Aaron predicts *stronger* without hesitation. This analysis of Aaron's miscues reveals the problem solving he continuously engages in as he reads.

Miscue Analysis: Rationale and Background

To avoid a pejorative view of error, Kenneth Goodman coined the word *miscue* to refer to readers' unexpected responses to written text (K. Goodman 1996a). Miscue analysis examines such responses. Some teachers and others who listen to children read call miscues *errors* and consider them in negative ways, believing that the teacher's role is to correct children in order to eliminate all errors. However, after a half century of miscue analysis research and practice, there is no doubt that ALL readers make miscues and that reading development CANNOT occur without them (Brown, Goodman, and Marek 1996). Often, miscues occur as a result of readers' knowledge about language, the content of what they are reading, and the problem-solving strategies they use for predicting and comprehending. The term *miscue* suggests that readers engage in making sense of what they are reading, intelligently selecting cues from the text based on their background knowledge and understandings. This sometimes leads them to read something other than what a listener expects to hear. Hence, the term *miscue*. However, miscues often produce a meaningful text. We call these *high-quality miscues* to celebrate the reader's ability to attend to the text's meaning.

That miscues reveal readers' capabilities makes professional as well as common sense. In all walks of life, we know that humans learn from their mistakes. We have mistakenly believed that if teachers do not correct, errors will be reinforced and students will continue to make them forever. Careful miscue analysis, however, shows that we should trust children's learning processes: miscues change over time even within the same story (as with Aaron's reading of *strong*, *born*, and *liked*), and they reveal readers' abilities to learn from the text as they read (Meek 1997). Miscues become more sophisticated as readers develop their reading strategies.

Kidwatchers are aware that the more they understand the nature of the miscues their children make, the better they are able to support their reading development. The ultimate goal of miscue analysis is to help teachers learn to listen to children read with educated *miscue ears*, to thoughtfully evaluate miscues and use miscue analysis to discover readers' *strategies*, which include

▶ monitoring reading in order to construct a meaningful text

▶ predicting or making educated guesses that make sense based on prior knowledge and comprehending of the text

▶ confirming and self-correcting miscues that do not make sense using grammar and phonic cues

▶ reading without overly long hesitations and pauses

▶ omitting words or substituting nonwords to keep reading

▶ using pictures and illustrations selectively

Teachers also are able to judge the degree to which readers are using their knowledge of language cueing systems by

▶ noting whether substitutions are the same part of speech, and fit the grammar and the meaning of the sentences in the whole story or article

▶ recognizing the extent to which omissions and insertions result in acceptable sentences

▶ evaluating substitutions that reveal knowledge of spelling patterns and phonics

▶ documenting the many sentences and words that the reader never miscues on

How Miscue Procedures Support Children's Growth

Kidwatching teachers use miscue analysis to help them understand how young readers are *making sense* and to observe them in the *process of constructing meaning*. They listen to children read a whole story or article without interruption because they know that when students are permitted to work out their strategies, teachers discover their ability to learn from the text. Each child's reading in individual conferences, in small groups, or during whole-class read-alouds provides information about the child's proficiency in reading.

In this section we provide vignettes of children's reading to show what teachers learn from these interactions, how they respond to the children, and how they use what they learn to inform their reading instruction. Sometimes, we place the published text next to the student's oral text, and in a few cases, we show what the typescript looks like when the teacher marks the miscues.

Miscue Analysis for Individual and Group Instruction

Nellie, a first grader, is reading the book *Days with Frog and Toad* (Lobel 1979). Nellie is familiar with Frog and Toad stories but has not read this one before (Meyer 1992, 60).

Ms. Kelly, who is listening to Nellie read, regularly tapes her students for miscue analysis purposes. She uses what she learns from the analysis to decide on specific strategy lessons for individual readers and to plan for small-group instruction.

After reading the thirty-eight-sentence story, Nellie retells it, and she and Ms. Kelly have an animated discussion about kite flying. By analyzing each sentence, Ms. Kelly knows that the majority of the sentences Nellie read made sense in the story, and this was more true at the end of the story than at the beginning. When she produced an unacceptable miscue (like *bail* for *ball* in sentence 5), she almost always corrected. Ms. Kelly notes that Nellie attended to meaning using graphophonic information as she disconfirmed and self-corrected her prediction of *bail of string* for *ball of string*.

Ms. Kelly decides to involve Nellie in listening to a section of the tape of her own reading (see Figure 6–1) in order to discuss with her the kinds of successful reading strategies she is using. For example, Ms. Kelly discusses with Nellie that although her miscues in sentence 2 result in an unacceptable sentence, she recovers not by self-correcting but by producing an independent sentence starting with *There* on the next line. She then engages Nellie in considering what she could have done to make the sentence acceptable. They then discuss how Nellie transforms sentence 5 so that it makes sense even though it doesn't fit well with sentence 6.

FIGURE 6–1 Nellie's Reading

Ms. Kelly understands that the words *said* and *and* sometimes pattern in a similar place in a sentence connecting two proper nouns (*"Toad," said Frog* and *Toad and Frog*), which may have caused the prediction and substitution of *and* for *said* in sentence 5. In addition, *said* and *and* look alike in the middle of the words and sound alike at the end. Ms. Kelly documents that Nellie read *said Frog* a number of times without miscues prior to and after sentence 5.

Ms. Kelly makes a note to discuss the particular *"Toad," said Frog* structure during her next guided reading session with the class. She realizes that in most texts for beginners, the word *said* preceding or following the proper noun (*"Toad," said Frog* or *Frog said, "Toad"*) usually comes at the beginning or end of the dialogue. The use of *said Frog* in this sentence occurs in the middle of the dialogue. This is more complex than her students are used to. Kidwatchers understand that reading is not just word-oriented but includes knowledge of grammar and meaning. Ms. Kelly will point out to the children the use of such dialogue carriers and have them explore the surrounding punctuation, which is another linguistic clue for them to use in such contexts.

Miscue Analysis for Whole-Class Discussion

Mr. Howard, a second-grade teacher, uses miscue analysis with his children during read-aloud time when it is appropriate. In this setting, he makes a miscue as he sings a new big book, *I Had a Little Overcoat* (Y. Goodman 1998), to his students. When Mr. Howard sings *vest* for *jacket*, Maralee and Renee, who still are not reading independently, say in unison, "That's jacket, not vest." Mr. Howard smiles at the children and continues to the end of the song. He then returns to the page on which he made the miscue and says: "Maralee and Renee noticed that I sang *vest* for *jacket*. They were paying careful attention. Why do you think I did that?" The students discuss that they are both things to wear, that Mr. Howard was anticipating the vest that was on the next page, that there is an E and a T in both *jacket* and *vest*. Whenever a child notices that he makes a miscue, Mr. Howard takes advantage of the situation to engage his students in considering the role of miscues in reading. After the children share their ideas, he asks, "Did it make sense in the story?" and "Did it sound right?" He likes to use his own miscues first to demonstrate that miscues are reflective of good thinking and that good readers make miscues. He then discusses students' miscues that other children notice in similar ways, being sensitive to the confidence of the readers. He wants the students to un-

derstand the positive nature of miscues, to wait for each other in the same way he waits to give them opportunities to engage with the text, and to realize that all readers, even good ones like teachers, make miscues. Mr. Howard demonstrates wait time whenever he reads with students, and helps them know that miscues show the understanding that readers have as they are reading. His demonstrations provide his children with ways to respond to each other when they are doing buddy reading or reading a book together in a small or large group.

Miscue Analysis for Children Who Need Extra Support

Ms. Hood meets with her primary multiage students regularly to evaluate what they do while they read. Although she trusts that her children learn from transaction with the texts they read, she carefully documents the strategies they use so she can help those who need additional support (Hood 1992, 57).

The Text:	**Jo Reads:**
We went up the track and the rain came down.	Once yup the tent and the rain comes doen (rhymes with *own*)
We put up the tent and the rain came down.	How puts yup the tent and the rain comes don't . . . down.
Dad cooked a meal and the rain came down.	Dad cooked a mill and the rain comes down.

Ms. Hood notices seven-year-old Jo's effective reading strategies but is concerned that she does not realize that everything that she reads must make sense. When Jo finishes reading, she tells Ms. Hood, "I didn't like this story. It didn't make sense. The words were silly." Ms. Hood documents what Jo knows about reading (we include examples that are not illustrated here): She is using initial sound-letter correspondences in almost all of her miscues (mill/meal; people/paddled; tent/ track; swimming/stream; keeps/came). She sometimes includes middle (comes/came; out/ our; swimming/stream) and ending (of/off;

mill/meal) sound-letter correspondences. She shows other understandings of graphophonic relationships as well. Her miscue of *once* for *we* in the first line shows that she knows that the beginning sounds of both words are the same. In her miscue *yup* for *up*, she is using the beginning sound of the letter U, which is the same as the sound at the beginning of other words that start with the letter Y, such as *you* and *yellow*. She substitutes *doen* and *don't* for *down*, taking into account sounds that can represent the first two letters of down and perhaps being aware of the pronunciation of *own*. And the part of her reading without miscues also shows her graphophonic knowledge.

However, Jo does not focus on meaning and seldom corrects. As a result of her miscue analysis, Ms. Hood works with Jo and a small group of students who have similar miscue patterns for a few days a week over a number of months. She selects materials that have familiar context, repeated natural language, and clear illustrations. As they read with each other, Ms. Hood asks them a number of questions: What could it say? What would you say there? Does it make sense? and How do you know? She supports the children so they share their reading strategies with each other to show how they attend to the text. Ms. Hood reports that when she used the same story at the end of the year, either Jo's miscues made sense in the story or she self-corrected the ones that did not. When she finished reading and retold the story, she said enthusiastically, "Hey! That story makes sense now!" and then connected what she was reading to a personal experience of camping with her family.

Miscue Analysis for Proficient Readers

Vincent is in first grade. His teacher knows that he is reading most narratives well. During reading time in class, Mr. Flurkey walks around, doing over-the-shoulder conferences. He notices that Vincent is reading a nonfiction book with more complex concepts and language structures than he usually reads in narrative texts. The book is called *Why Frogs Are Wet* (Hawes 1987). As Mr. Flurkey passes Vincent's desk, he hears him say to the other kids at the table, "I'm going to read this book *Why Are Frogs Wet?*" noting that he miscued on the title. Mr. Flurkey decides to let Vincent read for a while and return to listen to him later. When Mr. Flurkey returns, he sees that Vincent is reading on page 10, and he says, "Keep reading from where you are now, but read aloud and I'm going to listen and take some notes." (See Figure 6–2.)

When Vincent finishes the rest of the page (the text in Figure 6–2 plus three additional lines), Mr. Flurkey says, "Do you know what you read in the first line for this (points to *skin*)?"

Vincent responds, "Yes, I think I read *scales*, but there's no L or S. I saw that word a lot on the pages before, but I skipped it be-

FIGURE 6–2 Vincent's Reading

cause I couldn't make it out. Then I thought that fish breathe through their scales. Finally I thought that must be *skin* and I read it here (points to *skin* on third line) and it worked for the rest of the story. I just never thought that animals could breathe through their skins."

Mr. Flurkey asks Vincent to go back and find the places where he skipped *skin* and see if it works there, too. Vincent turns back the pages and reads each of the sentences with *skin* in it without miscues or pauses. Mr. Flurkey then asks, "So what are the smart things you did in your reading to decide that was *skin?*"

Vincent says, "Well, first I just skipped it and kept reading. I kept saying to myself, 'I wonder what that means?' and finally I figured it out. Now, when I went back to look at the sentences with the word *skin*, I got them. I guess I just never thought about skin being wet and breathing through your skin. When I read this sentence (points to a previous sentence: *The frog breathes through the pores in his skin.*), I read *puddles* for *pores* and that's why *skin* didn't sound right there. But when I knew it was *skin* then I knew this was *pores*. I know that pores are those little holes in my skin."

Mr. Flurkey follows with, "What else could you do in these situations when you are reading alone and silently?"

Vincent sums up, "Well, this book was a little hard, but I'm really interested in frogs so I kept thinking to myself, 'What does this mean and how can I make sense out of it?' "

Vincent's reading flows easily when he is comprehending. When he comes to sections of texts he is not sure about he slows down and hesitates, but he is usually able to work things out. He is still young and inexperienced and needs support, especially when he isn't making sense and "short-circuits" by deliberately omitting words, or by not correcting sentences that do not make sense. Mr. Flurkey involves Vincent in a conversation to help him evaluate his reading by articulating the strategies he uses successfully. Mr. Flurkey uses this critical teaching moment to help Vincent consciously inquire into his own reading process, and to encourage him to continue using the reading strategies that work well for him.

Now that we see how teachers use miscue analysis to understand their children's reading abilities and to lead to instructional strategies, we provide information that will help you use miscue analysis when your students read. A number of procedures are used for miscue analysis. The material we provide here includes information that a teacher needs to document and analyze, but it does not include information available in other miscue analysis procedures. As you become aware of the power of miscue analysis, we encourage you to become familiar with alternative procedures that examine in greater depth the degree to which students use reading strategies and language cueing systems. Additional information about miscue analysis procedures can be gleaned by taking a course or by reading *Reading Miscue Inventory* (Goodman, Watson, and Burke 1987) or Sandra Wilde's book on miscue analysis (2000). These and other readings are listed in the references at the end of this book. It is important to keep in mind that by being involved in careful observation and analysis of your students' reading, you will continue to build your understanding of the reading process, to develop ways to use this knowledge to evaluate your students' reading, and to plan for relevant instruction.

How to Document and Analyze Miscues

The procedures in the following sections provide suggestions for formal record keeping and anecdotal note taking. In *formal miscue analysis*, the teacher tapes the child's reading and retelling, listens to it again, and analyzes the miscues and retelling, resulting in a Miscue Analysis Kidwatching Profile. It is helpful to do a formal miscue analysis on children at the beginning and end of the year and to read regularly with them, taking anecdotal notes, the rest of the time. For those readers who need greater support in developing proficient reading, it may be helpful to carry out alternative miscue analysis procedures (see Bibliography).

Formal Miscue Analysis

Formal miscue analysis involves audio- or videotaping a child's oral reading of a complete story or article followed by a retelling or other kind of presentation. We believe that the use of reading strategies is generally similar in silent and oral reading but that there are important differences teachers should be aware of. In silent reading the reader does not need to perform for an audience and is usually more confident in taking risks. However, by listening thoughtfully to children while they read orally, we gain insights into their concern for making sense while they are reading.

The teacher needs the following materials for formal miscue analysis:

▶ a complete story, book, or article that is new to the reader (see the upcoming section on selecting materials)

▶ a summary outline of the story/book/article to use during the retelling (see the upcoming section on retelling)

▶ a typescript of the complete reading material that is formatted to look like the original and is double-spaced

▶ a tape recorder with a blank tape

The teacher usually sits next to the child and says, "I'm taping your reading so that we can listen and talk together about the kinds of things you do when you read and how you develop as a better reader during the year." The teacher also reminds the child, "Remember that I won't help you while you are reading because I want to be able to talk to you about what you do when you are reading alone. After you finish reading, I will ask you to retell (or sketch) what you have read."

One of the most powerful results of miscue analysis is learning how to listen to children read by staying on the sidelines rather than immediately giving them words or telling them what to do when they get stuck. Football coaches do not get on the field with their players; they stay on the sidelines. We have discovered that the more we support readers by encouraging them to rely on their own reading strategies, the more they develop their abilities to rely on their own resources. As teachers relinquish the power of being a corrector, it is amazing to watch children develop their own problem-solving strategies.

During the reading, the teacher marks the miscues on the typescript and also notes observations such as finger pointing, subvocalizing, and use of pictures as well as other relevant comments. If the reader stops reading for an extended time (more than thirty seconds), the teacher asks, "What can you do to keep reading?" and supports the child in talking about the various strategies he or she can use (see Mr. Flurkey's interactions with Vincent earlier in this chapter). Following the reading, the teacher asks the reader to retell the story (see the upcoming section on retelling). If the reader was reading a nonfiction article or book, the teacher suggests that the reader discuss the main concepts, or make a sketch, diagram, or time line.

Teachers listen to the tape after the reading to double check the miscues they recorded during the reading. They mark on the typescript all differences between what they expect to hear and what the reader reads. They document in the following ways:

▶ substitutions—Write over the substituted words. Note Vincent's *scales* for *skin* on line 1 and Nellie's *and* for *said* in sentence 5. (See Figures 6–2 and 6–1, respectively.)

▶ omissions—Circle omissions. Note Vincent's omission of *of* on line 2 and Nellie's omission of punctuation and *I* in sentence 5.

▶ insertions—Use a caret (∧). Note Vincent's insertion of *the* before *land* on line 2 and Nellie's insertion of a period in sentence 2.

If the reader repeats or self corrects any section of the text, the teacher underlines the whole segment of repeated line (see Vincent's repetition of *through his* and Nellie's repetition of *bail of string*). If the repetition results in a correction, the teacher marks it with a ⓒ (see Nellie's miscue of *bail of string*, which was repeated and self-corrected in the process). If the repetition is an unsuccessful attempt at correction, the teacher marks it with a ⓤⓒ (Aaron's attempts at reading *strong* in the sentences on pages 4 and 6 were marked with a number of underlines and a ⓤⓒ on his marked typescript since his substitution of *soft* was still an unsuccessful attempt; see page 62). If the repetition of the phrase is without miscues, the teacher marks it with an ⓡ, as noted in the last line of Vincent's reading. Such marking gives the teacher insights into the repetition strategies readers use in order to keep comprehending the author's work. Overly long pauses (more than five seconds) are marked with an elongated P for *pause*, as shown in line 3 of Vincent's reading. Vincent's pause and repetition suggest that he is wondering about the substitution miscue he made on line 1 (*scales* for *skin*).

What is most important in miscue analysis are the quality of the miscues and the overall pattern of their use in constructing a meaningful text, rather than the quantity of miscues or the nature of a single miscue. In most cases as readers learn to make higher-quality miscues and are more confident in their reading, their number of miscues diminishes. The quality of miscues is judged by the degree to which miscues sustain the meaning of the text. We make those judgments by reading each sentence including the miscues as the reader finally resolves them and asking a series of questions about each sentence and the miscues in the sentences:

Does the sentence the reader finally produces make sense in the story or article? Here we examine semantic acceptability to see which miscues retain the meaning of the story or article and which disrupt it. We note the strategies the reader uses in comprehending or making sense of the text, such as

predicting and confirming. We examine self-correcting strategies in relation to those miscues that disrupt meaning. When readers self-correct high-quality miscues too often, it is a sign that they are paying more attention to the surface of the print than to the meaning.

An example of a miscue that results in a semantically acceptable sentence is Vincent's insertion of *the* before *land: On the land a frog breathes through his lungs and his skin.* He did not correct this miscue because it made sense in the story. When he omitted *of* in *He takes air out of the water*, the result was a semantically unacceptable sentence. Therefore, he self-corrected and his final reading of the sentence was fully acceptable. However, his miscue of *scales* for *skin* results in a sentence that is not semantically acceptable because frogs do not have scales. The teacher makes note that although Vincent makes omission miscues on *skin* earlier in his reading, and reads *scales* for *skin* in one context, he reads *skin* appropriately in all the subsequent occurrences. Also, the initial sound-letter correspondences are similar and there is some meaning relation between the two words. In discussing this miscue with Vincent, the teacher learns more about his comprehending strategies and supports him in his problem-solving strategies.

Does the sentence the reader finally produces sound like language? Here we examine syntactic acceptability to see the degree to which the reader is concerned that the reading sounds like language. Sentences that are semantically acceptable, are always syntactically acceptable, but there are times when readers produce sentences that are syntactically acceptable but do not have meaning in the story. For example, even though Vincent's reading of *scales* for *skin* is not semantically acceptable in this text, it is syntactically acceptable because he predicted a noun for a noun.

There are also times when readers make up nonsense words that have the same part of speech and the same number sense as the original words in the text. One example is Aaron's reading of *warrr . . . um tongue* for *warm tongue.* When he came to this word in the previous sentence, he deliberately chose to omit it. The second time he read the word, he used a sounding-out strategy and produced a nonword that resulted in a syntactically acceptable sentence that was not semantically acceptable. His intonation pattern made clear that he was reading an adjective and noun at the end of the sentence. Using this placeholding strategy of producing a nonword in this context supported Aaron's comprehending because at the next occurrence of *warm*, he did not miscue.

Do the miscues in the sentence change the meaning of the story/book/article? Here we note the extent to which the miscues in each sentence have changed the meaning of the story/book/article: to a great degree or only in a minor way. Aaron's and Vincent's sentences show that many of their miscues result in little change in meaning, especially after using repetition and self-correcting strategies. Proficient readers often make miscues that do not change the meaning at all. However, the last sentence that Jo reads (see page 65) results in a major meaning change (*Dad cooked a mill and the rain comes down*).

Do the reader's substitution miscues show that the reader is using phonics or graphophonic knowledge? Here we examine the degree to which the miscues have similar patterns to the words in the text. We note that Nellie's miscues such as *bail* for *ball* and *there* for *where* have high graphic and sound similarity, while *log* for *large*, *made* for *meadow*, and *and* for *said* show some graphic and sound similarity. When we take into consideration that the rest of her reading is without miscues, we are able to document that Nellie uses her phonics and graphic knowledge when she reads. We examine all the miscues to see if there are any recurring patterns (miscues on all words that start with *wh*, for instance) in order to plan individual strategy lessons for readers who produce such patterns throughout a reading.

When readers have a high percentage of graphophonic similarity, we examine the miscues to see whether the reader shows a pattern of producing miscues that overuse graphophonic strategies at the expense of meaning. Such readers have a high number of nonwords or have low-quality substitution miscues that do not result in acceptable sentences but have high graphic and sound similarity. In such cases, we know that the reader is more concerned with the sound-alike and look-alike quality of letters and the shapes of words and less concerned with paying attention to meaning. Such readers are using inefficient and short-circuiting strategies, and their instruction needs to include strategy lessons that focus on making sense while reading in addition to attending to the graphophonic cueing system.

For formal miscue analysis, we produce a Miscue Analysis Kidwatching Profile and Summary (see Figures 6–3 and 6–4 at the end of the chapter). These are record-keeping forms that include information about some of the questions in this section. You will find explanations about how to complete the forms and analyze and interpret the miscues on pages 74–75.

Informal Miscue Analysis

Informal miscue analysis can occur whenever a teacher listens to a child read. The teacher notes children's miscues while they are reading at their desks, during buddy reading, or during read-alouds. The children may be reading books, newspaper articles, or other materials.

The teacher keeps in mind the same questions that were listed earlier for formal miscue analysis but typically takes notes on sticky notes or cards that she keeps for each child:

▶ Do the miscues in the sentence make sense in the context of the story (semantic acceptability)?

▶ Do the miscues result in a sentence that sounds like language (syntactic acceptability)?

▶ Do the miscues in the sentence change the meaning of the story/book/article and to what degree?

▶ Does the miscue show that the reader is using graphophonic knowledge (graphophonic cueing system)?

▶ Does the miscue need to be corrected (predicting and confirming strategies)?

The teacher notes information about the reading strategies and cueing systems the child is using proficiently, and how they relate to each other. She considers the specific instructional support each child will receive during individual conferences based on the miscue patterns that show the child's needs. She uses the Kidwatching Profile and the Kidwatching Profile Summary (see Figures 6–3 and 6–4) to summarize the information she collects on the individual child. She also makes notes about general strategy lessons that she will plan for guided reading, small reading groups, or whole-class discussions.

Conducting Retellings

Retellings are always a part of miscue analysis because they enable children to share their comprehension of the story. With formal miscue analysis, teachers often have a set of stories and articles set aside that their children are not familiar with (see "How to Choose Appropriate Materials"). They prepare outlines for the stories so that they are able to follow along easily as the child retells. It helps with the retelling for the teacher to be familiar with the story but at the same time to keep the child's view of the world in mind. The child takes the lead in response to a request such as "Tell me everything you remember about the story." After the child finishes the unaided retelling, the teacher moves to an aided retelling using the outline to ensure that the key components of the story/book/article are addressed. But the questions the teacher uses remain open-ended. For example, if the child mentions the grandfather from the story, the teacher may request, "Tell me more about

the grandpa." In this questioning, the teacher uses the child's language, not the book's language. If the child calls a character Robbie instead of Roberta, as it was in the book, the teacher uses the child's choice of name in further questioning. In this way, the teacher finds out if the child has developed character awareness even if he or she isn't sure of the pronunciation of the name.

During retelling it is important to use wait time so the child has time to think about what happens in the story or article. If the child says, "I don't know," or "I don't remember," we often respond with "Just say a bit more about (whatever the child has said)," or "Close your eyes and see the story in your mind and tell me more." Or, we might ask general questions such as "Where did the story take place?" "How are the characters like people that you know?" or "What happened after (an event the child mentioned)?" Sometimes, we ask the child to retell the story to one or more of his classmates or to pretend that her or his best friend is there. Retelling information may also take the form of diagrams, sketches, or a written review, especially if the material does not lend itself to a traditional narrative retelling. With a piece of artwork or writing in hand, the teacher then asks the child to talk about what she or he drew or wrote.

The Kidwatching Profile and Summary forms include a place to document retelling information (see Figures 6–3 and 6–4). Any diagrams, drawings, or writings can be stapled to the form. The teacher indicates whether the retelling and other responses were thorough and complete or whether the child gave an appropriate synthesis or summary. In addition, the teacher notes inferences or misconceptions that reveal the reader's background knowledge and experience, and uses this information to plan ongoing instruction. It is important to remember that a strong summary statement indicates good comprehension; it is not always necessary for the child to retell every detail in order. It is interesting that when sequence is important to the plot of a story, children relate it easily, but when sequence has no importance, what happens first and then next is not something children remember. If you or your children have not done retellings before, it is important to keep in mind that both you and the children will get better at the process with more opportunities to do so.

With informal miscue analysis procedures, retelling is informal as well. The teacher follows up book or article discussions by extending the child's conversation. This may occur one-on-one, or during literature groups or whole-class discussions. The teacher documents the child's comprehension and knowledge about the reading on sticky notes or in the summary section of the Kidwatching Profile.

Keeping Cumulative Records

From the vignettes we used earlier, it is obvious that the teachers are taking notes or analyzing miscues that they keep in each child's cumulative folder. A cumulative folder is different than the child's work folder, which contains self-selected artwork and writing and is kept in consultation with the child. The cumulative folder provides a place for the teacher to keep a record of the child's literacy learning history, and it is passed along with the student during her or his school career. The material in the folder provides a wealth of information to use for reporting purposes and the teacher shares the information with the child, the parents, other teachers, and administrators whenever it is appropriate to do so. The folder includes

▶ profile sheets that show in-depth analysis of the child's reading and writing miscues

▶ anecdotal records and informal notes

▶ lists of books and other materials to document the child's silent reading

▶ retellings, responses, and other presentations (drawn and written)

▶ reading interviews

▶ interest inventories

▶ test score data

▶ beginning/mid/end-of-year self-evaluations

▶ the child's reading and writing goals

▶ the parents' goals

How to Choose Appropriate Materials

For formal miscue analysis, the teacher must know her students in order to select material. Teachers who regularly use miscue analysis organize a *miscue materials collection* that includes a rich selection of fiction and nonfiction materials that can be used by students with a wide ability range. These are materials that the teacher does not usually use within other parts of the curriculum so that the materials are not familiar to the readers. Although the specific material for formal miscue analysis should be new to the reader, the language and the content should be familiar. Margaret Mooney (1998, 1990), a New Zealand educator, suggests that all reading material must have appeal to the children: the content must be worthwhile and authentic, and the language must be effective and spark the imagination with memorable phrases. There is no simplistic way to judge reading difficulty. Readability formulas and leveled books based on word counts and simple grammatical structures do not take into account the knowledge and interest of any reader. When we understand the nature of miscues, we discover that readers often are willing to struggle with a text that is above the level of an arbitrary test of accuracy. Important learning occurs when readers build confidence in their ability to take risks with more complicated materials. When we use leveling devices for texts, we do not have the opportunity to discover the strategies and knowledge that readers are capable of using. In addition, we find that too large a diet of simplistic, single sentence per page stories sometimes is harder for the readers who need the most support. Therefore, the miscue materials collection should include a range of reading material of different genres to challenge and interest all the readers in your class.

Children should also be involved in learning to self-select their reading materials, and discussions with students about reading difficulty should become an important part of instruction. Many children are reluctant to choose materials and rely on teacher judgment; many have misconceptions about grade-level materials. When teachers discuss with children what makes reading material easy or hard, and develop with them criteria for choosing materials, they gain insight into children's views about reading difficulty, and children become more independent in exploring a range of materials. During informal over-the-shoulder conferences, listening to buddies reading together, and during classroom read-alouds, the miscue analysis takes place using the materials the children are already reading.

Some Final Thoughts About Miscue Analysis

We encourage you to share what you are learning about the reading process during individual conferences and class discussions with your children. A number of the vignettes in this chapter demonstrate the ways in which conversations with students support them in becoming consciously aware of the reading process. When we share with students what we are doing and learning during miscue analysis, and invite them to self-reflect on their reading process, we learn even more. Currently, we are exploring such teacher and student conversations with readers of all ages through retrospective miscue analysis (Goodman and Marek 1996). We are learning that by talking about their own reading with other children and the teacher, children become consciously aware of the good strategies they are using and of the strategies they are using that may interfere with building comprehension. Such information, when developed through student self-reflection and inquiry into their own language and thinking, helps children become more confident and take

more risks while they are reading. They build a language to talk about their reading and are able to apply their ideas to new reading experiences. It is helpful for teachers to continue to develop ways to hold such conversations with their students.

It is important to remember that miscue analysis is based on oral reading. However, we want to make clear that children should be encouraged to engage in silent reading, continuously practicing and applying the strategies they develop during oral reading instruction and conversations. We use oral reading in miscue analysis because we can't crawl into the children's heads to observe what is happening as they monitor and engage with written text. However, the bulk of reading that we do in our lives is done silently, and children need a lot of opportunities to engage in silent and personal reading. Talking with children about what they think they are doing when they read silently gives us an additional window into their reading processes.

Finally, miscue analysis has many benefits in addition to evaluating your children's reading abilities. As we mentioned at the beginning of this chapter, it is a professional development tool for teachers because each miscue analysis teaches us new things about the reading process and about readers. It is important for teachers to be patient with themselves as they explore miscue analysis and to be open to new learnings. Whenever we do a miscue analysis, we are amazed at what we learn about children's knowledge about language and reading. A psychologist once said, "The only road to experience is through inexperience." Teachers need to keep this in mind not only for their children but for themselves. We know that through miscue analysis, you will discover new knowledge and insights that come with delving into the reading process and discovering new ways to work with your students. The most common statement we hear from teachers after they have completed at least five miscue analyses on their children is "I will never be able to listen to children read in the same way that I used to."

Explanations for Miscue Profiles

A. *Comprehending Information*: This information reflects the reader's construction of meaning during the reading of the text. No single sentence or miscue provides information about a reader. It is the pattern of problem-solving strategies that readers use throughout a reading that is important to note and examine.

Code YES (semantically acceptable) each sentence the reader reads with the following patterns:

▶ The reader makes no miscues in the sentence.
▶ The reader produces substitution, omission, or insertion miscues that retain the sense of the sentence.
▶ The reader self-corrects all the substitution, insertion, or omission miscues that do not make sense.
▶ The reader produces substitution miscues that make sense but have no graphic or sound similarity.
▶ The reader's intonation indicates that the language of the story has been rearranged but the shifts result in sentences that make sense.

Code NO (not semantically acceptable) each sentence the reader reads with the following patterns:

▶ The reader produces miscues that do not make sense and does not self-correct.
▶ The reader produces substitution miscues that look and sound like the word in the text but do not make sense and the reader does not correct.
▶ The reader produces nonword substitution miscues that retain the syntax or grammar of the sentence.

The teacher places the number of YES and NO responses on the profile form and calculates a comprehending score following the directions. A score of 70 percent or higher suggests that the reader is concerned with making sense. By reviewing the miscues in the sentences, the teacher documents the prediction strategies and the ways in which the reader uses self-correction strategies. As a result of examining this question, the teacher gains insights into the background knowledge and confidence of the reader.

B. *Grammatical or Syntactic Knowledge*: Some of the sentences that readers produce are not semantically acceptable, but they sound like language and retain the grammatical structure of the sentence. It is important (especially with second language learners) to document such sentences because they reveal readers' knowledge of the grammar of language, and their capabilities to produce syntactically acceptable sentences. Readers often substitute the same part of speech (e.g., a noun for a noun) or rearrange sentences in a way that maintains their grammatical acceptability. They also show their knowledge of letter-sound correspondences as they substitute appropriate prefixes (*about* for *around*) and suffixes, even on nonwords (*proposely* for *purposely*). In addition, listening to readers' intonation patterns reveals their control of the grammatical information in sentences. Although the goal is to help the reader make sense of the text, grammatically acceptable sentences are a mark of readers' strengths and show that they are using language cues even when they are unfamiliar with certain words or phrases. Many authors, like Lewis Carroll, play with language when they produce nonsense stories or poetry. Our young readers are producing the same kinds of inventions.

In addition, examining syntactic knowledge provides teachers with information about the reader's unfamiliar concepts. For example, in sentence 2, Nellie reads: "*They went to a log made.*" She probably predicted that a noun should follow the word *a* when she read *log* for *large*, using her phonics knowledge of initial and medial sounds. But *meadow* was unfamiliar and the result was a grammatically unacceptable sentence. However, her intonation showed that she ended the sentence after *made*. She then started the next line with *There*, an appropriate sentence beginning, to substitute for *where*. This last part resulted in a sentence. She also showed her syntactic knowledge when she produced miscues in sentence 5 and transformed Frog's dialogue into a declarative sentence. The shifts of first-, second-, and third-person singular in this section of the story may have been somewhat complex for Nellie to handle; however, she showed a strong sense of grammatical knowledge as she rearranged these sentences to result in syntactic acceptability. The teacher writes the examples of such sentences on the profile form to note changes over time and to use for instructional purposes.

C. *Phonics and Graphophonic Knowledge*: Evaluating the similarity between substitutions and text words provides information about readers' knowledge of phonics as well as the degree to which readers are aware of the graphic or look-alike quality between their miscues and text words. Although we gather this information by examining only substitution miscues, it is important to remember that all words without miscues have been read with graphophonic knowledge. We find that readers who are proficient and readers who are less proficient do not differ much in graphic and sound similarity scores, especially since high-quality substitutions often do not look or sound like the word in the text (*Daddy* for *Father* or *job* for *work* are examples).

A combined score of *High* and *Some* graphophonic similarity of 65% (or more) indicates that the reader is using graphophonic information most of the time. We code the look-alike quality of the miscues by asking, To what degree does the substitution look like the word in the written text? If two out of three of their parts look alike (the beginning and middle or the beginning and end), we code High similarity. If one of three parts have letters in common (the beginning, the middle, or the end) we code Some similarity. Most miscues fall into these two categories. If there are no letters or sounds in common, we code these miscues as No similarity. Often words with no similarity are semantically and syntactically acceptable in the sentence because the reader is using good prediction strategies, so we list these on the kidwatching profile. Such miscues occur more in the reading of proficient readers. The profile sheet provides space for the number of high and some similarity, and indicates how to compute a percentage score for each category. Checking recurring patterns of specific features of miscues provides evidence for individual strategy lesson instruction. This same analysis can be done by asking the sound-alike question: To what degree does the substitution sound like the word in the text? With this question, the teacher must keep the child's dialect in mind. For example, what the teacher hears as a substitution of *rowed* for *rolled* may simply be the way this child from New Jersey says *rolled*. Other common examples include what sounds like *offen* for *often* or *axed* for *asked*. Such dialect variations are not coded as miscues.

D. *Repeated Miscues*: Examining repeated miscues shows readers' problem-solving strategies when the same word is repeated more than once in the text. This examination provides additional information about readers' comprehending strategies throughout the reading of a text. It provides the rationale for a reader reading a whole text without specific help. Repeated miscues show readers' predictions as they adapt strategies across the text and problem solve to figure out the author's intention. The teacher notes the text word and indicates the number of times the same word is read or the kinds of changes the reader makes. It is interesting to note that when the miscue is a high-quality one, proficient readers usually stick with the same miscue (often true for name substitutions), but if the miscue doesn't work very well, they try various responses using all the language cueing systems to produce something that is eventually successful. Less proficient readers often produce new miscues each time and make less use of semantic and syntactic information than proficient readers do.

E. *Retelling Information*: The notes teachers take during the retelling provide evidence of the reader's comprehension of the story/article. This section can be used for both formal and informal miscue analysis to include comments about the retelling and note the language the reader uses to retell. Inferences show the reader's ability to understand the underlying meaning of the written material. In making an inference, readers combine their prior knowledge with information provided during their reading to construct new meanings that are not mentioned explicitly in the text. A major misconception provides evidence of concepts readers hold that do not match the author's intentions and suggests that the child would benefit from a specific strategy lesson to expand on the concept. A holistic score can be calculated by using a 1 for high, to indicate that the reader provided a very complete retelling, to a low of 5, to indicate a minimal retelling.

The *Kidwatching Profile Summary* may be used with either formal or informal miscue analysis. It provides a place to summarize the miscue analysis on one page to see at a glance the child's strengths as well as his or her needs. The summary also includes comments about the reader, the reading, and the retelling and includes a section for listing strategy lessons and noting reading strategies and other aspects of reading instruction for each child. Caryl Crowell, a primary grade teacher who uses this form, says that she is better able to plan when she can take into consideration at one time the interrelationships of the reader's knowledge of the language cueing systems, his or her strategies, and his or her retelling. Caryl also uses the summary to record additional reading behaviors she observes during the child's reading such as the use of picture clues, finger pointing, subvocalization, body movements, and comments the child makes while reading. The information on the form is also useful for comparing summaries—and therefore, progress—across time.

Reader _____ Age/Grade_____ Date_____

Teacher _____ Selection _____

A. *Comprehending Information*

Does the sentence with or without miscues after the reader has finally read it make sense in the story/article? Mark YES on the typescript next to all sentences without any miscues; sentences with miscues that make sense; and sentences where the unacceptable miscues are self-corrected. Mark NO next to the unacceptable sentences. Then fill in the following information:

1. Number of sentences in the story/article. Total Number: _____
2. Number of sentences marked YES. Total Number: _____
3. Divide total number in 2 by total number in 1 to get percent of sentences in story/article that are semantically acceptable or make sense. _____%

B. *Grammatical or Syntactic Knowledge*

Number of sentences that do not make sense but maintain grammatical structure: _____

List typical examples:_____

_____

_____

_____

_____

_____

C. *Phonics and Graphophonic Knowledge*

1. Total # of word-for-word substitutions: ____   # of High Similarity: ____
   # of Some Similarity: ____
2. Divide # of High/Some by total substitutions.   High Similarity: ____%
   Some Similarity: ____%

List examples:

High Similarity   Some Similarity

_____for_____   _____for_____

_____for_____   _____for_____

_____for_____   _____for_____

_____for_____   _____for_____

List miscues with no similarity and circle Yes or No, depending on whether they result in acceptability within the story/article.

_____for_____ Yes No   _____for_____ Yes No

_____for_____ Yes No   _____for_____ Yes No

_____for_____ Yes No   _____for_____ Yes No

D. *Repeated Miscues* (List the same word that is miscued on more than once during the reading.)

Text Word: List each substitution and/or omission and number of each occurrence:

_____   _____

_____   _____

_____   _____

_____   _____

_____   _____

E. *Retelling Information*

The retelling provides evidence of the reader's comprehension of the story/article. Circle the statement that is most applicable: Plot/General Idea   Complete   Some   Minimal
Supporting Details/Events   Complete   Some   Minimal

Inferences (Indicate major or minor.):

_____

_____

_____

_____

Misconceptions (Indicate major or minor.):

_____

_____

_____

_____

_____

_____

Reproducible, see p. 113   Reproducible, see p. 114

FIGURE 6–3   Miscue Analysis Kidwatching Profile

List statistics and relevant comments.

Semantic Acceptability (the degree to which the reader is comprehending or making sense)

Yes____% No ____%

Examples for discussion purposes:

_____

_____

Syntactic Acceptability (the degree to which the reading sounds like language)

Examples for discussion purposes:

_____

_____

Graphophonic Similarity (the degree to which the reader is using phonics and graphophonic knowledge)

High____% Some ____%

Examples for discussion purposes:

_____

_____

Meaning Change (Examples of miscues that change the meaning.): _____

_____

Retelling (Use child's language to document comprehension.) Holistic Score ____

_____

_____

_____

_____

_____

Comments about the reader and the reading:_____

_____

Plans for strategy lessons and other reading instruction: _____

_____

Reproducible, see p. 115

FIGURE 6–4   Kidwatching Profile Summary

Writing

Amelia is interviewing Cayla for a biography she is writing.

CAYLA: [*speaking in phrases to give Amelia time to write*] When I got older—

AMELIA: [*writing*] *When . . . she . . . got . . . older*—because someone else is writing it—*When she got older . . . she went to kindergarten* . . . Okay, how many friends did you have?

CAYLA: Put twenty-three. [*Amelia writes a T.*] Wait—just write the number. [*Amelia writes 23 F-R-A-S.*]

CAYLA: Fras?

AMELIA: *Friends.* I just sounded it out, but it's in our books so I can get it [the conventional spelling] later.

Hard at work on a biography, these first graders illustrate the extraordinary complexity of writing development. Rather than developing one concept at a time, they are simultaneously developing control over many aspects of written language. To be effective, flexible writers, they must develop knowledge about written language functions, formats, and genres; they must understand the roles of narration and audience; they must develop control over orthography, phonology, and punctuation; and they must develop a *positive sense of themselves as writers.*

In one sitting, Cayla and Amelia are doing just that. First, they are exploring what written language is for. In this case, its *function* is to document and share with an audience the life and history of an individual. Second, they are exploring how written language is organized. Given their purpose, the most suitable *format* seems to be a narrative and the sensible *genre* choice a biography. Third, they are exploring how to get words and ideas on paper. Their knowledge of the relationships between *orthography* (the written system of language) and *phonology* (the sound system of language) enables them to invent spellings, and also to include some words they already know how to spell. Fourth, they use *punctuation*—in this case, word spacing, periods, and capitalization—to convey their intended meanings. Finally, Cayla's and Amelia's *positive sense of themselves* as authors is shown in their willingness to exchange writing ideas, and in their confidence that they will be able to create a meaningful text. As children engage in meaningful acts of writing, they develop numerous concepts about writing simultaneously. As we move through the chapter, we will look more closely at each of these concepts and offer guidelines and suggestions for their evaluation. Before we begin, it is important to note that children develop writing at the same time as they develop reading. One doesn't come before the other. In fact, throughout the early childhood years, writing, reading, and talk develop simultaneously, with each supporting the development of the others.

Written Language Functions

Five-year-old Davonte's baby sister is almost out of diapers. "Davonte," his mother requests, "write a note and put it by the keys so we don't forget to stop at the store."

Two-year-old Chloe brings a pretend grocery list to four-year-old Aster (a store worker). Aster unfolds it and looks at it: "Let me read it. All right, we'll give you that."

Six-year-old Ryan carefully draws and cuts out a series of cards and badges that contain the pictures and names of his favorite cartoon char-

acters. Throughout the afternoon, he uses them to reenact what he has seen on television.

As families engage in daily events such as running errands, preparing meals, going shopping, and seeking entertainment, they use written language to serve a variety of functions. In the vignettes, Davonte and his mother use a note as a reminder to stop at the store; Chloe uses a list to remember what to buy when she goes shopping; and Ryan uses pencil and paper to re-create an imaginative and entertaining world. For young children, knowledge of functions is important because it provides the foundation for all literacy exploration. When children know what written language can do for them, they want to use it, and they want to learn to use it conventionally. If children do not understand why we use written language, then there is little reason for them to read or write.

Kidwatching teachers know that children's knowledge about written language functions (both writing and reading) reflects their unique sociocultural experiences. It is for this reason that they support and encourage varied kinds of writing—kinds that may be unplanned for or unanticipated in a school setting, but which are meaningful from the child's perspective. When children have agency to write in ways that reflect their social and cultural experiences, their potential to show us what they know is expanded. In ideal composing settings, students' childhoods are present in their activity (Dyson 2001), and it is in ideal settings that kidwatchers document what they know.

Following is a set of questions to consider as you observe children's writing and as you evaluate and plan curricular experiences.

1. What functions of written language are familiar to my students? What functional knowledge do they demonstrate during play; freewriting times; choice times? Consider the following:

> *Environmental print* provides information about the world around us. Examples are

found on street signs, store signs, book jackets, schedules, bills, price tags, and coupons, and in advertisements, instructions, directories, and reference books.

Occupational print is used to do one's job. Children see occupational print in the workplace, and sometimes in their homes. They often bring it into their play. Examples of occupational print include receipts, forms, health records, appointment books, menus, recipes, order pads, signs, email messages, and money.

Informational print is for storing, organizing, and retrieving information. Examples are found on calendars, clocks, cubbies, diagrams, receipts, and boxes of materials, and in biographies, laptop computers, encyclopedias, newspapers, and telephone books.

Recreational print is used for leisure activities. Examples are found in videogames, storybooks, poetry books, television books, magazines, movie critiques, the-

ater bills, and travel brochures (Whitmore and Goodman 1995).

2. How does literacy development occur through children's exploration of functions? What can I do to enhance this development?

3. What materials are available (and necessary) for students to demonstrate and expand their knowledge of functions?

4. What functions do I value and support most? How do my values inhibit or expand the children's exploration?

Written Language Formats and Genres

As teachers evaluate children's knowledge of written language functions, they also evaluate their knowledge of written language formats and genres. Format and genre are closely interrelated. *Format* refers to the "shape," or configuration, that written language takes when it is used to serve a specific function. Erica's example in Figure 7–1 shows that a list is a good format choice when we need to

FIGURE 7–1   Erica's Birthday List (My Birthday List: a big stuffed dog, a toy cash register, a doll locker, a hamster cage, a remote control Barbie gymnastic set)

remember or record a bunch of things—it's brief, concise, and all that's needed to effectively accomplish the task. *Genre* refers to a category of language that classifies both format and content. If a list is a format, then a birthday list is a genre, because it has both a specific format and content. Children who have opportunities to use written language to serve a variety of functions develop important knowledge about formats and genres. For example, they learn that email and letters are formatted differently than stories, and they contain different kinds of information; lists and schedules are formatted differently than newspaper articles, and they contain different kinds of information.

The examples we have included in this chapter illustrate that as children use reading and writing for real purposes, they have opportunities to develop knowledge about genres—their content and form. This knowledge is important to readers and writers because it informs the meaning-making process. For example, when Erica's five-year-old brother reads her birthday list, he will use his knowledge about format and content. He knows the piece of paper will contain items his sister likes, and that they will be presented in a list format. Such knowledge gives readers clues to what the words might say, guiding their predictions and expectations. Writers use genre knowledge, too. Knowledge of genre helped Erica to efficiently organize her work and to produce a text that meets reader expectations. In these ways, knowledge of genre fosters communication.

As teachers observe children's writing, they do so with an eye for the genres they are exploring. Just as they do with reading, they want to make sure that children are exploring a variety of genres in their writing. But, they also watch for the ways in which children invent unique genres to meet their communicative needs. Figure 7–2 lists some functions, formats, and genres to look for and encourage as children work and play in your classroom, but keep in mind that these are only a starting point. Let children explore in open-ended

ways, and they may surprise you with their creations. Over time, teachers watch for children's uses of genre to expand, and within each genre, for their pieces to become longer, more coherent and cohesive, and structurally more complex (Dyson and Freedman, 1991).

Orthography and Phonology

As writers are developing knowledge about written language functions, formats, and genres, they are also developing knowledge about the ways in which the orthographic (written), phonological (sound), and graphophonic systems work. *Graphophonics* refers to the systematic relations between patterns of letters and

_____ Advertisements	_____ Observational notes
_____ Alphabet books	_____ Nonfiction in varied genres
_____ Announcements (birth, death)	_____ Pamphlets
_____ Autobiographies	_____ Phone messages
_____ Bills	_____ Plans for events
_____ Biographies	_____ Poems and songs
_____ Blueprints	_____ Posters
_____ Book jackets	_____ Price tags
_____ Calendars	_____ Programs (for theater, events)
_____ Cartoons and comics	_____ Receipts
_____ Charts and graphs	_____ Recipes
_____ Checks	_____ Records of events
_____ Computer software/publishing programs	_____ Reports (weather, sports, scientific)
_____ Coupons	_____ Requests for information
_____ Diagrams	_____ Restaurant orders
_____ Expressions of opinion	_____ Reviews (of books, movies, TV shows)
_____ Forms	_____ Rules
_____ Health records	_____ Schedules
_____ Instant messaging	_____ Scripts
_____ Instructions (for games, crafts)	_____ Self-evaluations and reflections
_____ Internet search engines	_____ Signs
_____ Invitations	_____ Stories (in varied genres)
_____ Journals and logs	_____ Tickets
_____ Labels	_____ Webs
_____ Letters, email, notes, and cards	_____ Word puzzles and games
_____ Lists	_____ _____
_____ Maps	_____ _____
_____ Menus	_____ _____
	_____ _____

Reproducible, see p. 116

FIGURE 7–2   **Written Language Functions, Formats, and Genres**

patterns of sounds. In the following sections, we show how kidwatchers use samples of children's writing as "windows" into their orthographic, phonological, and graphophonic knowledge. However, before we proceed, we want to point out that although our focus in the following pages is on analyzing the surface features of writing (such as spelling) we believe that teachers best support children when they focus first on meaning.

Orthographic Knowledge

Children discover the orthographic system as they experiment with reading and writing, and as they participate socially in literacy events. Orthography includes the configuration of letters, directionality, punctuation (including segmentation), and font. One of the first discoveries that children make about the orthographic system is that there is a difference between drawing and writing. Those squiggly symbols that adults call letters are much more than shapes or designs; they actually represent language. When children discover that print carries linguistic meaning, it shows in their writing and drawing. For example, in Figure 7–3, three-year-old Antonia drew a carrot, wrote her name (an A and some

Ns), and then wrote the series of small shapes while saying, "I . . . played . . . with . . . the . . . car . . . rots . . . I . . . played . . . with . . . the . . . car . . . rots."

Antonia's example illustrates that, early on, writers may surround or superimpose their picture with invented characters and letter-like forms, or write them all over the paper. Over time, they develop awareness that print proceeds in a linear fashion (in English usually from left to right and top to bottom), and they begin to use this directionality principle in their writing. Aster's restaurant order in Figure 7–4 and Karla's plan for play in Figure 7–5 provide examples of children who have developed the concept of directionality.

Aster's and Karla's writing looks like that of many beginners. Aster uses an invented cursive style: "closed or open curves—linked together by a wavy line." Karla uses separate characters "composed of curved and/or straight lines" (Ferreiro and Teberosky 1982, 180). Although they haven't yet discovered conventional letter forms, they are attending to the way print looks. Although children's early forms of cursive and print aren't readable to adults, and aren't even readable to the writers soon after they're written, we call this

FIGURE 7–3   Antonia's Carrot

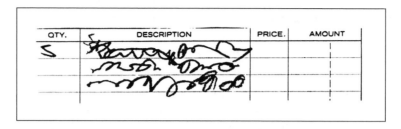

FIGURE 7–4 Aster's Restaurant Order: Invented Cursive

writing because it is intended to communicate meaning.

Antonia's and Karla's examples show that many young writers initially use sets of characters—circles, squiggles, lines, crosses, or letterlike forms—that are similar in shape (OoOOo). As they continue to see print in their environments, they notice that the letters in most strings vary (O+O++), and they begin to apply this criterion to their own writing. Early writers also develop a sense for what a word looks like. Their written words, even when using invented symbols, begin to look like real words in terms of their length (usually a minimum of three letters) and internal variation (no using a character more than twice in a row) (Ferreiro and Teberosky 1982; Schickedanz 1999). As they observe their students write, teachers document these early discoveries.

The first conventionally spelled words that many children write are their own names and the names of other important people in their worlds. But, many children are still not alphabetic at this point. They know how to form the letters, and often write them in the appropriate order, but they still have not discovered that certain letter patterns represent certain sounds (the alphabetic principle). Instead, they see each word as a unique representation of a person, object, or thing. To them, a word is much like an icon or a logographic symbol on a computer or street sign. However, name writing is important, even when it does not draw on alphabetic knowledge. Many children use their own names and the names of the people they know as a linguistic pool of knowledge to support them as they hypothesize rationales for the ways in which letter strings are organized, and as they

FIGURE 7–5 Karla's Play Plan: Invented Print

begin to search for specific letters to represent specific sounds.

Figure 7–6 provides a framework for collecting information related to children's early knowledge of orthography in a formal setting. It also provides a way to collect information about their knowledge of written language functions, formats, and genres.

Interpreting the Child's Concepts of Written and Pictorial Representation

To make sense of the information gained from the Written and Pictorial Representation assessment, teachers ask themselves a set of interpretive questions. These questions help them develop insights into the child's understandings and plan instruction that is in tune with what the child knows.

▶ What knowledge does the child demonstrate about the differences between drawing and writing?

▶ Does the child believe that he or she can create meaning through writing?

▶ Is the child willing to pretend to write and read?

▶ What modeling and support might encourage the child to take risks in these areas?

Name: _____ Date_____ Grade_____

Procedures: Offer a variety of paper and writing utensils. The italicized phrases are suggestions to use to engage the child in writing. Ask the child to respond to each item, document all verbal and nonverbal responses, and save the child's drawing and writing (or a copy), recording the date, the context, and any other pertinent information.

1. Offer the materials and encourage the child to *Write something.* If the child declines, suggest that he or she *Pretend to write.*

2. *Read me what you wrote.* If child says, "I can't," ask why, and then suggest that the child *Pretend to read.*

3. *Tell me about what you wrote. What are this and this?* (Get at the terms *word, letter, sentence, period, question mark,* and so on.)

4. *Write a letter.* (Children may respond with an alphabetic letter or write a letter to someone.)

5. *What do you write at home?*

6. *What do you write at school?*

7. *Why do people write? What kinds of things do they write? Can you write (or pretend to write) any of these things?*

8. *Draw a picture.*

---

9. Make sure the child is looking directly at his/her writing and drawing.

  a. *Show me your writing. Show me your drawing.*

  b. *Is drawing the same as writing?*

  c. *How are they alike (the same; like each other)? How are they different?*

10. Enlarge the following samples to fit on a single sheet of paper or cut each apart to fit on separate cards. Ask the child *Which of these are writing? Why do you think so?*

bread	n'est-ce pas?	⇨	T5A28B
go	✈	〰〰〰 〰〰〰	K
FFFFFF	*kitten*	📫	piñata
●❖⊠⌘	Get on the bike.	**RESTROOMS**	▼△◄▷ ◣◥

11. Invite the child to write his/her name. *Do you know how to write any other names?*

12. Write three different-looking names including the child's and ask him/her to point to his/her name and read it.

Adapted from Y. Goodman (1992)

FIGURE 7–6   Concepts of Written and Pictorial Representation

▶ What kinds of symbols does the child use to represent meaning (pictures, invented letters, conventionally formed letters, numbers)?

▶ What sense of directionality does the child show?

▶ What understanding of the concept of a word does the child show? Do the child's words look like real words in terms of length and internal variation?

▶ What linguistic terminology (*letter*, *word*, *period*) is familiar to the child?

▶ What knowledge does the child demonstrate about the functions/formats/genres of written language? How can I provide opportunities for further exploration of these (and new) functions/formats/genres?

▶ What knowledge does the child have of name writing and reading?

▶ What phonological knowledge does the child demonstrate? (See next section.)

Phonological Knowledge

Families and teachers delight when children gain control over the phonetization of written symbols—when they begin to use letter patterns to represent sound patterns in conventional ways. Teachers document growth in this area by collecting writing samples over time and using anecdotal notes to remember what the children's invented spellings were intended to communicate.

Understanding that letter patterns systematically relate to sound patterns is a major step toward being able to communicate through reading and writing. When children develop this understanding, we say they have developed the *alphabetic principle*, or have become *alphabetic*. As alphabetic children begin to invent spellings for words, they may use only their most prominent sounds. Often, prominent sounds are consonants, and many children include only the initial or the initial and final consonants in their spellings of

words and syllables (in English). Vowels and vowel markers (used when two vowels work together to make a sound) typically show up later (Wilde 1992). For example, when Cory wrote his first response to literature in early September of his first-grade year, he used one symbol to represent almost every syllable. As he was writing, he said the words slowly, sounding like this: *Lla-mas ea-tuh pa-ja-mas* (Llamas eat pajamas). Following is the result:

L	Z	E	T	B	Z
Lla	mas	ea	tuh	pa	ja	mas

Cory's example illustrates that he is exploring the alphabetic hypothesis, and also the *syllabic* hypothesis. Children who are syllabic hypothesize that each spoken syllable corresponds with each letter in a piece of writing. It is important for teachers to keep in mind that bilingual children will reveal different patterns of representation. Spanish-speaking children, for example, typically use vowel letters prior to including consonant letters in their invented spellings.

Throughout September, Cory did what children typically do as they develop more control over the alphabetic system: he began to represent more specific units of sounds in his writing. For example, late in September, he wrote a get-well card:

I	HP	U	G	B	T	SN
I	hope	you	get	bet	ter	soon

By late October (only four weeks later), when he wrote a report about snakes, his invented spellings reflected even more explicit units of sound (*rdalsnack* for *rattlesnake*), as well as a beginning pool of high-frequency words, such as *do* and *get*. (Some teachers call these sight words.)

DO NTO GET NEAR A BAD ANAMEL LIC A RDALSNACK
Do not get near a bad animal like a rattlesnake.

Cory also showed awareness that many words are not written like they sound. For example, he spelled *near* conventionally, either because he had developed a visual memory for the word or because he was developing more sophisticated phonics knowledge (using *ea* or *ear*). He also showed that he realized that English spelling often incorporates a vowel in every syllable.

Figure 7–7 shows some of the key strengths that kidwatchers look for as they document their students' spelling knowledge. Although some developmental trends are evident, children often explore several of these aspects of invention/spelling at the same time, and have been observed to move back and forth between them (Graves 1983; Read 1975; Wilde 1992).

Punctuation and Other Orthographic Knowledge

Punctuation is another element of the orthographic system that is of interest to teachers.

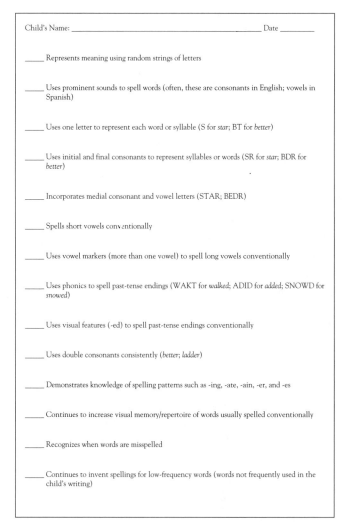

Reproducible, see p. 119

FIGURE 7–7 Spelling Knowledge

As with all aspects of written language, children test hypotheses about punctuation, and can be expected to invent forms of punctuation as they are needed to express various meanings. In talk, meanings are expressed through intonation, gesture, pauses, facial expressions, volume, tone, and other shared cultural understandings. Because these devices are not available in written language, writers use punctuation and other visual features.

Punctuation serves two general purposes. First, it serves to segment linguistic units (sentences, phrases, and words). Segmentation is achieved through such devices as spaces, line breaks, commas, and periods. Children usually use spaces and periods before they explore other punctuation. Second, punctuation serves to highlight meaning. Meaning is conveyed through such devices as question marks and exclamation points. Variations in font, bolding, all capitals, or shifts in letter stylistics also serve to highlight meaning. Children explore these elements of punctuation early in their writing development when they want to show emotions (l♥ve), noise (POW), or power (**KEEP OWT!**)

Documenting children's development of punctuation and other orthographic features is especially interesting because the field has limited information on how this knowledge develops. In general, as children gain experience with writing and reading, teachers observe the ways in which they become increasingly aware of orthography and effective in using it as a signifier of meaning.

Children's orthographic knowledge develops in concert with their phonological knowledge. For example, word spacing is one of the first forms of punctuation that children explore. (Although not written, spaces are a distinct form of punctuation. Like periods and commas, they serve to segment written language.) Some children initially do not include spaces between words. Then, realizing the need for segmentation, they may try a variety of symbols between words—periods, squiggles, dashes, commas, lines, or circles. Finally, they discover that spaces serve to segment written language. Such discoveries are made as a result of writing in a social environment, as well as through rich experiences with reading. Knowledge of punctuation and orthography develops as children observe their uses in varied kinds of texts, intuit the need to include them in their writing, and explore ways of incorporating them into their writing. By examining these features in addition to spelling, kidwatchers discover the constructive or inventive nature of children's exploration of the writing system.

Control Over Multiple Symbol Systems

A final aspect of writing to document is the ways in which children go about constructing meaning, or their processes of getting ideas on paper. Development in this area is characterized by children gaining progressively more control over numerous processes. When the youngest children write, their meanings are created through much more than print itself. Meaning is made as children weave together writing with talk, drawing, movement, and sound. For example, four-year-old Joshua, writing and drawing a story, provides a play-by-play account of the events experienced by the main character (a "circus guy"), tells his peers what his letterlike symbols mean, makes howling sounds, and rattles his paper for special effect. Although not yet able to produce a readable text *per se*, even very young children create meaningful messages through the use of multiple symbol systems (Dyson 1989; Graves 1983). Joshua's example illustrates why many young children are more interested in the processes than the products of their writing, and also why it is enlightening to observe young children's inventions *as* they write.

While observing children write, teachers document the ways in which they use multiple symbol systems to shape and share their imagined worlds. *Talk* is perhaps central within these systems. Children as young as three may use talk to rehearse for composing, to narrate what they are writing, to provide the play-by-play action of their drawings, and to clarify their intended meanings. Talk used in these ways often elicits feedback from others, helping children to develop a sense of audience and to extend their knowledge and thinking. Children also use talk to solve specific problems of encoding and composing. They talk about story ideas, wonder about titles, sound out words, check spellings, discuss punctuation, and reread to determine whether something makes sense or sounds right. In general, talk supports children in getting their ideas on paper, sharing their creations with others, and solving their specific problems of encoding, with each of these supporting their overall development. Organizing writing centers, peer conferences, collaborative writing experiences, and time for writing with others on the computer provides rich talk opportunities for children to talk through all kinds of ideas. In some preschools, teachers tape butcher paper over a whole table and place a canister of various writing implements in the center. Children come together to talk at "the writing table" as they explore the drawing and writing systems.

Drawing serves purposes similar to talk. Drawings help children rehearse and develop ideas for writing; supply information about characters, settings, and events; and disambiguate text; and they help others understand what has been written. Drawings may also be more accessible to peers than writing, and may therefore elicit more responses (Dyson 1989; Graves 1983). Many teachers have observed that less experienced writers use drawing differently from those who are more experienced. For example, six-year-old Piper draws an elaborate picture and then reflects, "I draw first because then I know what to write about." Her eight-year-old sister, Ivy, tells her story before writing it down, and then adds a small, less detailed drawing to the page. A comparison of Piper's and Ivy's strategies typifies development in general: as children gain experience with composing, many begin to draw after writing. Their pictures begin to function more as an illustration for the product than as a rehearsal for the process, and they often become less detailed as children's words begin to carry more meaning (Sowers 1985). As children gain experience with composing, they do not abandon drawing, but instead begin to use it more deliberately, having gained a more deliberate control over that which they convey through pictures and that which they convey through a written text (Dyson 1989).

In general, kidwatchers expect children to use multiple symbol systems to make meaning as they write. They don't insist that children must write first or draw first, but instead help them discover which serves their purposes best. Most children move from a reliance on a number of symbol systems to a steady incorporation of more and more meaning into the print itself. Their development, therefore, is characterized by a resolving of the tensions among symbol systems, or as a differentiation between the information conveyed through written text and that which is conveyed through social activity (Dyson 1989). Over time, teachers document the changes in children's talk, drawings, and use of other symbolic media.

Children also begin to internalize problem-solving processes (such as sounding out a word aloud or representing emotional tones in their writing) that they had initially explored orally and through social collaboration. However, when a writer is producing a first draft or trying something new, or when a piece proves difficult to write, the use of external symbol systems for solving problems may reappear (Sowers 1985). As writers attend to new concerns, their attention may be directed at those concerns, resulting in the temporary neglect of already-developed conventions. Also, as children become more aware of the relationships between oral and written language, and specifically, more aware of the alphabetic nature of written language, they may become tentative about what they can do and may even become unwilling to write. Knowing what they don't know can make things appear to be falling apart. However, kidwatchers know that writing development is recursive, and that tentativeness is a part of development. They expect to see writers reconfiguring and backing up as they expand and develop their knowledge, and they support their students in doing so.

Because social activity is so central to writing development, kidwatchers ensure that children have many opportunities to write with others—and they observe them as they do. As you observe your students writing in various genres, the following questions will help you focus on their meaning-making processes:

▶ What meaning is the child assigning to his or her writing?

▶ How does the child use varying symbol systems (drawing, talk, movement, sound) to express meaning and solve problems while writing?

▶ What social and cultural knowledge is reflected in the child's writing?

▶ What is the nature of the child's social activity while writing?

▶ How can I use this information to support the child's development as a writer?

Identity as a Writer

As all of these exciting aspects of development are taking place, teachers observe their students' developing writing identities, or the ways in which they are coming to see themselves as writers. As we discussed in Chapter 2, identities influence how children approach literacy events and, therefore, how they continue to grow and develop.

Depending on children's experiences, some come to see writing as something that offers entertainment, clarifies thinking, provides a way to socialize, and provides a tool for their own empowerment in the classroom and in society. Some come to see writing as a tool for creating a more equitable society and culture. For example, they learn to document instances of classroom gender bias and use this information to confront bias in a direct, systematic way; or, they learn to write letters to authors and publishers as they encounter racial or class stereotypes in the literature they read. Children who feel the power of writing and feel positive about themselves as writers are likely to want to write, and to make an effort to learn to communicate effectively in writing. Children who come to see their writing as something that is not neat enough, not conventional enough, not connected to their lives, or not meaningful in the real world are likely to be unmotivated to write, and if their experiences are negative, they may avoid taking the risks that are requisite to their growth. Obviously, classroom writing experiences have a tremendous influence on children's writing identities. Children develop a strong and positive writing identity when they write for meaningful purposes and when they feel comfortable enough to take the risks that allow them to express themselves through varied genres.

Guidelines for Evaluating Writing

As they evaluate, teachers focus on developing insight into both the processes and the products of children's writing. To organize their observations, they make a plan for observing children as they write and for collecting meaningful writing samples.

Observing Children as They Write

As we have illustrated, young writers simultaneously develop knowledge about written language functions, formats, genres, orthography, phonology, punctuation, grammar, and processes for getting ideas on paper. Figure 7–8 lists these aspects of development with space for anecdotal note taking. The items listed on the form can be used to create an overall profile of the child as a writer. Each aspect of writing listed is important but cannot be evaluated each time the child writes. Instead, different aspects are evaluated over time (using anecdotal notes and writing samples) and dates and contexts are recorded.

Child's Name: _____ Date _____	
What to Look For	Examples and Instances
Knowledge about the functions of writing (e.g., uses writing for varied purposes; writes on varied topics; explores functions in play; knows when to use a list, web, envelope, note, card, sign)	
Knowledge about written language formats and genres (e.g., writes in varied genres; uses different forms; uses typical generic features; invents new features)	
Knowledge about ideas and content that are expressed in writing (e.g., content is connected to personal life and classroom inquiries; content fits the format and genre; humor and sensitivity develop in appropriate genres)	
Knowledge about orthography and phonology (e.g., forms letters; understands that print means; knows difference between drawing and writing; represents written language syllabically; shows alphabetic knowledge)	
Knowledge about punctuation (e.g., explores use of spacing, line breaks, periods, commas, question marks, capitalization, dialogue markers, font variations)	
Knowledge of grammar (e.g., sentences are complete in narrative; words or phrases are used appropriately in specific genres; dialogue is used)	
Processes of getting ideas on paper (e.g., solves problems collaboratively; asks for help; invents spellings; copies items around the room; uses pictionary or dictionary; uses private speech; uses talk, drawing, movement, and sound)	
Social processes (e.g., works collaboratively with others; talks about writing; sensitively and thoughtfully responds to others' ideas; conferences; participates in author's chair)	
View of self as writer/author	

Reproducible, see p. 120

FIGURE 7–8   Note-Taking Form for Observing Writing

Collecting Writing Samples

As kidwatchers evaluate children's writing processes, they carefully evaluate their products. To do so, they develop a system for collecting writing samples over the course of a school year. Most kidwatchers, in collaboration with children, keep dated samples of writing in a work folder for each child. Some of these samples may come from home. At the end of each week, they invite children to select one piece of writing to keep in the folder. All other pieces are taken home. At the end of each month, they discuss with the child the growth that has taken place, and together, they choose one or two samples to leave in the folder for the year.

In addition to this, many teachers collect a formal sample from each child every month. They arrange for either the whole class or small groups to write for five- to thirty-minute sessions (depending on their age, interest, and willingness to stay involved) in response to some prompt. The prompt may be open-ended or teacher-directed and may be focused on curricular issues or on children's personal interests and areas of knowledge. Some examples follow:

Open-Ended Prompts
(Leave choice up to the student.)

▶ You may write on this paper.

▶ Let's think and talk about things we like to do. (Teacher or children record the possibilities.) Tomorrow, I will ask you to write about one thing that you like to do.

▶ Write anything you'd like about a real person. It could be a person you know from your own life, or a person you have heard about or seen on television.

▶ Write a story about anything you wish. Today you may plan (draw, sketch, talk, make a web); then, for the rest of the week, you will have time to write.

▶ Write something that will teach your audience about something you know a lot about.

Teacher-Directed Prompts
(Provide opportunities for choice/ connection to student interest.)

▶ Today, talk with your author study group about all the things you have learned about Patricia Polacco and her books. Use this time to plan to write what you have learned. Tomorrow, you will write about what you have learned.

▶ Think about what you have learned about pets since we began our science theme study. This morning you will have time to think about what you

would like to write and organize your thinking either by drawing, taking notes, making a web, or using other techniques you know. You may work with your partner. Then, for the rest of the week, you will have time to write.

▶ Dr. Mays (the principal) is curious to know what we did on our trip to the nursing home yesterday. Write a description of everything we did.

▶ Develop one or two characters, and then use them to write a story that incorporates some of the key elements we have learned are found in fairy tales.

Evaluating Processes and Products

Evaluating children's writing is a process that is unique to each classroom. The first step is to consider what *you* need to know in order to help *your* students expand their developing competencies and to provide a record of their growth. We find it helpful to collect data that allows us to answer the following questions:

1. How does the child feel about writing?
2. What does the child know about writing?
3. What do the child's unconventional uses of writing reveal about his or her knowledge?
4. How does the child rehearse for writing? What topics is the child selecting?
5. In what settings does the writer seem most involved and engaged?
6. What are the child's areas of expertise?
7. What genres does the child prefer?
8. Which pieces are most clear and complete? What are the topics? What are the genres? In which settings were they produced?
9. In what ways does the child collaborate with others during writing time?
10. How can I use this information to help the student expand his or her competencies?

Some teachers supplement such questions with a checklist or profiling form that is directly tailored to the needs of the children in their classrooms. For example, the areas in

Figure 7–8 are useful to consider in examining each child's selected samples. These forms are reproduced and kept in each child's work folder, along with writing samples that provide evidence for what is listed on the forms. Figure 7–9 provides an example of a profiling form prepared for a kindergarten classroom.

As you collect samples for the work folder, it is important to keep in mind that because writing development is not a linear process, it is unlikely that each new piece will show improvement. As children try new genres, explore new strategies, experience new tensions, and place their focus in new areas, their knowledge seeking may appear random; it may meander and seem to regress, yet at other times, it may leap forward, ultimately showing new constructions and understanding.

Supporting Student Evaluation

Children in kidwatching classrooms learn to evaluate their own writing as they work with peers and teachers. Sometimes, this occurs through the daily discussion and collaboration that happen as children write; other times, it occurs as children participate in conferences with peers and teachers. Conferences ensure that focused time is devoted to identifying children's strengths and needs.

As we have suggested before, self-evaluation is the most important kind of evaluation. Self-evaluation helps children to know and articulate their strengths. Children who are aware of what they can do develop confident identities as writers. They are willing to use and share their knowledge, and to take the kinds of risks that support further

Child's Name: _____ Grade_____						
Knowledge Demonstrated:	Sept	Nov	Jan	Mar	May	Description/Examples/Reflections
Draws to signify meaning						
Uses invented characters to signify meaning						
Shows a sense of directionality						
Uses random strings of letters to signify meaning						
Writes letters to represent beginning or prominent sounds						
Writes letters to represent vowels and medial consonants						
Is beginning to conventionally spell commonly used words						
Uses spacing between words						
Uses capitalization for names and places						
Writes sentences with appropriate grammatical form						
Uses simple punctuation (.?!); more complex punctuation (",')						
Chooses own topics for drawing and writing						
Writes with sensitivity						
Explores varying voices (serious, informative, humorous)						
Shares pictures and writing with others						
Rereads own writing/revises/edits						
Explores multiple genres						
Self-evaluates						

Reproducible, see p. 121

FIGURE 7–9   Profile of Writing Knowledge

- Discuss what the writer likes.
- Discuss what the reader likes.
- Discuss the author's use of pictures to support meaning.
- Discuss what the piece is about (reader goes first, to give writer a sense of the meaning that is being conveyed to the audience).
- Discuss whether the piece makes sense.
- Discuss whether the events are presented in a logical order.
- Discuss the formatting (as in advertisements, posters, poetry, brochures, signs).
- Discuss whether events are believable.
- Discuss whether characters seem real.

For writing that has been revised and edited and is ready for publication:
- Check spacing between words.
- Check spellings.
- Check capitalization.
- Check punctuation.
- Check paragraph breaks (narrative) or line breaks (poetry).
- Check for neatness.

FIGURE 7–10   Possibilities to Consider

learning. Self-evaluation also helps children identify their learning needs and develop a manageable set of goals for future learning. When children and teachers set one or two goals together, both are able to focus their attention on those goals. To support shared evaluation, some teachers create evaluation lists of "possibilities to consider" for the en-

tire class (using elements such as those featured in Figure 7–10). Items on such forms are first considered by the child, and then may be discussed between the child and the teacher or among peers. Many teachers find it most helpful to use a conference time to create individual criteria to support self-evaluation (as featured in Figure 7–11), rather than using a

---

Student's Name: <u>Salvador E.</u>

Instructions: Regularly collect pieces of writing over the course of the school year. With each, discuss with the student (1) the strengths of the piece; (2) the child's self-evaluation capabilities; and (3) joint goals for future learning.

Why did you choose this piece? What makes it good?	What kinds of things can you do to check your work?	What are one or two things you would like to work on?
9/27 Salvador chose this because he likes his picture. Says it's good because he wrote his name & didn't "mess up."	* Name * Date	Salvador seems very tentative/nervous. Decided not to ask this question.
10/25 Salvador says this piece is good because "It's long & about soccer and the pictures show a lot and there's lots of pages and I used periods."	* Illustrations match words * Periods and question marks * Everything makes sense	"Revising to be sure it makes sense." (When Salvador read it to class, J. said it didn't make sense.)
11/29 Likes it because it's creative and because he "wrote a problem in it that got solved and wrote periods & The End."	* Capital letters * Details	Writing about things he knows lots about. Use details and examples.
12/20 "I like to read it. It's really what we do for Christmas. I want to show my mama."	* Check spelling * Check lowercase as and es so easier to read	Using quotation marks.

FIGURE 7–11   Self-Evaluation Form

general self-evaluation form for the whole class.

As children learn to conference, a simple set of guidelines or ideas for discussion is helpful. When presented with an evaluation task, a long list can be daunting, and children may simply check off all items. Working with two to four items (at least initially) often results in more in-depth work on the part of the children. Such selective evaluation works for teachers, too. Figure 7–10 features some possibilities that may be used to help children get started. Figure 7–12 provides an example of a form used to guide peer conferences in a first-grade classroom. Such forms can be placed in large print on the classroom wall, or may be

reproduced and kept in each child's work folder.

Keeping Cumulative Records

Much of the writing data that kidwatchers collect is placed in a cumulative folder for each child. Cumulative records are different from the child's work folder, which is kept in conjunction with the child and contains self-selected pieces of writing, self-evaluations, and goals for future learning—anything you and the child might refer to regularly. (Many work folder items are placed in the cumulative folder.) The cumulative folder provides a place for the teacher to keep a record of the child's literacy learning history, and is passed on with the child from year to year. The cumulative folder may include

► writing samples (formal and informal)

► profile forms and checklists

► anecdotal records and informal notes

► lists of pieces written, their topics, and their genres

► writing interviews

► interest inventories

► beginning/mid/end-of-year self-evaluations

Conclusion: Expanding Repertoires

If you could be any kind of writer, what kind of writer would you be? What strengths would you have? Would you write to create a more just and equitable world? Would you write mysteries that keep readers on the edge of their seats? Historical fiction that carries people to other places and times? Poetry that moves people and helps them "see" in new ways? Newsy letters to extended family members? Jokes and riddles that make people smile? Religious materials that inspire kindness and goodwill? Music that makes people want to sing and dance? Technical material that teaches about something you know?

Writer: _____

Reader: _____

What the writer likes:

What the reader likes:

The writer will work on:

Reproducible, see p. 122

FIGURE 7–12 Peer Conference Form

Packaging labels that make products seem appealing? Advertisements that entice people to buy things? Brochures that describe travel adventures? Biographies of famous people? An autobiography or memoir of your own life?

Children in elementary school should have access to all of these possibilities—and many more. Your responsibility as a kid-watcher is to allow children meaningful opportunities for writing that draw from their social and cultural experiences and to help them explore new possibilities. The most informative kind of evaluation occurs as children are engaged in learning experiences that they find personally and culturally meaningful.

As we come to the end of our adventure into writing a book about kidwatching, we know that the very next time we walk into a classroom, we will have new suggestions about ways to observe children and ask questions about what they are learning. This process is never ending and is often exhilarating. Kidwatching not only gives us insight into children's language and literacy but it helps us learn more about language itself and how people learn it. As teachers share their learnings with one another, everyone benefits. We therefore invite you to share with us the questions, concerns wonderments, ideas and suggestions that you develop in your adventures as a kidwatcher. E-mail Yetta at ygoodman@u.arizona.edu and Gretchen at gowocki@svsu.edu. We will make every effort to pass on your new ideas and the questions you raise.

Appendix

REPRODUCIBLES

Detailed Observation Form

Getting to Know Your Child

Getting to Know Your Child's Language and Literacy Practices

My Child as a Language Learner: Parent Observation (Pre-K–1)

My Child as a Language Learner: Parent Observation (Grades 2–3)

Families in the Classroom

Evaluating Print Awareness

Child's Concepts of Reading

Informal Observation of Book Knowledge

Book-Handling and Print Concepts

Book-Handling Knowledge

Talk Contexts

Oral Language Functions: Classroom Observation

Oral Language Functions: Individual Observation

Interactional Competencies

Miscue Analysis Kidwatching Profile

Kidwatching Profile Summary

Written Language Functions, Formats, and Genres

Concepts of Written and Pictorial Representation

Spelling Knowledge

Note-Taking Form for Observing Writing

Profile of Writing Knowledge

Peer Conference Form

Detailed Observation Form

Child's Name: _____

Scheduled Observation Dates: _____

Settings Observed	Individual	One-to-one or Small Group (record which)	Whole Class
Reading/Discussing Print/Interests and Attitudes Toward Reading			
Writing/Discussing Classroom Writing/Interests and Attitudes Toward Writing			
Oral Language			

Figure 1–4, p. 10

Getting to Know Your Child

Dear _____,

This information is most helpful to me as I get to know_____ and you. Please send it at your earliest convenience. Thank you. (Use the back, if needed.)

1. What changes (health, maturity, interests) have occurred in your child's life this summer?

2. What areas of school life has your child especially enjoyed? (Or, what areas do you anticipate your child will enjoy?)

3. Toward what areas of school life has your child expressed negative feelings?

4. What does your child do well?

5. What goals do you have for your child this year?

6. In general, how is your child's self-concept? Does he/she believe in his/her abilities?

7. What special needs (academic, social, personal, linguistic) does your child have?

8. Where does your child go after school?

9. What are your child's favorite after-school or weekend interests and activities?

10. What else do you want me to know about your child or about you?

Adapted from Howard (1994)

Figure 2–1, p. 17

Getting to Know Your Child's Language and Literacy Practices

Dear _____,

This information will help me get to know_____ and you. Please return it at your earliest convenience. Thank you. (Use the back, if needed.)

1. What are some of the things your child likes to do and talk about?

2. What are some places your child visits frequently?

3. In what settings does your child talk most comfortably?

4. What language(s) does your child speak? What language(s) are spoken in your home? Does your child hear different languages at family gatherings or in the community?

5. Do you ever read with your child or other children at home?

6. What different languages do family members read and write?

7. What kinds of reading does your child participate in alone or observe at home? In what languages?

8. List any of the family's favorite books, authors, characters, cartoons, or videos.

9. Does your child ever read TV advertisements or captions?

10. Does your child ever use or play on a computer?

11. What are some things your child likes to write or draw when given a blank piece of paper? What other kinds of writing does your child do?

12. What kinds of reading or writing do you and other family members like to do?

Figure 2–2, p. 18

My Child as a Language Learner: Parent Observation (Pre-K–1)

Child's Name: _____ Date_____ Grade _____

Please tell me about your child's language learning in the following areas, and share examples where possible. If more than one language is spoken in your home or family, please include information about which language you are referring to. I appreciate your insights as we work together with your child.

My Child:	Usually	Sometimes	Rarely	Comments and Examples (If more than one language is spoken, let me know about your child's strengths in each.)
Speaks clearly so others can understand				
Is able to follow oral directions				
Enjoys listening to and telling stories				
Enjoys being read to				
Has favorite books, characters, magazines				
Understands stories we read aloud				
"Reads" to me (telling about pictures and/or the story)				
Helps with grocery lists, coupons, shopping, recipes, and so on				
Tries to read words in real contexts and settings (street/store signs, cereal boxes)				
Draws pictures and writes some letters				
Writes in invented spelling (makes up spellings for words)				
Likes to tell about what he/she writes				

At home my child enjoys:

I have questions about:

Parent_____

Adapted from Language Arts Committee, Palo Alto Unified School District (1994)

Figure 2–3, p. 18

My Child as a Language Learner: Parent Observation (Grades 2–3)

Child's Name: _____ Date_____ Grade _____

Please tell me about your child's language learning in the following areas, and share examples where possible. If more than one language is spoken in your home or family, please include information about which language you are referring to. I appreciate your insights as we work together with your child.

My Child:	Usually	Sometimes	Rarely	Comments and Examples (If more than one language is spoken, let me know about your child's strengths in each.)
Initiates and enjoys conversations with friends and adults				
Listens and responds appropriately to others				
Follows multistep directions				
Enjoys listening to and telling stories				
Enjoys being read to				
Has favorite books, characters, magazines				
Chooses to read independently				
Tries to read unknown words using meaning (good guesses), picture cues, or sounding out				
Can retell a story in own words				
Checks out books from school and public libraries				
Chooses to write independently (stories, poems, notes, lists, signs)				
Likes to talk about/share his/her writing				
Uses invented and correct spellings				

At home my child enjoys:

I have questions about:

Parent_____

Adapted from Language Arts Committee, Palo Alto Unified School District (1994)

Figure 2–4, p. 19

Families in the Classroom

To help make this school year meaningful for each child, we would like to invite family members to share their expertise with us. The following information will be useful as we plan the children's educational experiences for the school year.

What knowledge, guidance, or experiences would you like to offer to the classroom?

__ Work with children on projects (help them write, read, find information). Please let us know if you are able to support children in languages other than English.
__ Listen to children read. In which language? _____
__ Bring in a story to read. In which language? _____
__ Tell a story (personal, family, community, traditional, folktale).
__ Sing a song or play a musical instrument.
__ Share hobbies or work-related knowledge such as cooking, painting, car detailing, gardening, fishing, sewing, woodworking, secretarial, retail, and so on.
__ Share an object of interest from your home.
__ Demonstrate how you use technology in some part of your life.
__ Share a childhood game.
__ Teach about the languages you use.
__ I prefer to observe only.
__ Other_____

What sorts of home-school connection activities would you prefer?

__ Visiting the classroom during the school day.
__ Evening activities and workshops.
__ Child study groups (groups of parents discuss their children's learning).
__ Take-home activity packs.
__ Home-school journals (writing back and forth with the teacher).
__ Family-oriented homework (biographies, collecting family stories).
__ Personal notes or emails to and from the teacher.
__ Phone calls to and from the teacher.
__ Classroom newsletter.
__ Communication in languages other than English: _____
__ Other_____

Does anything make it difficult for you to participate in school activities?

__ Dates and times of school activities.
__ Conflicts with work.
__ Not comfortable speaking the language(s) spoken in the school.
__ Younger children at home (or others who may need care).
__ Not enough information (about the activities, dates, times).
__ Other _____

Your Child's Name: _____

Adapted from Owocki (2001)

Figure 2–6, p. 23

Evaluating Print Awareness

Child's Name: _____	Date: _____

Introduction

Ensure that the situation is comfortable for the student and then explain the procedures: *I have some things to show you, and I'd like you to tell me what you know about them.* Or, *I'm going to ask you some questions.*

Note whether student has had previous experience with the item:	*Have you ever seen this before? Where?*

1_____   6_____   11_____
2_____   7_____   12_____
3_____   8_____   13_____
4_____   9_____   14_____
5_____   10_____   15_____

Note student's response to the print:	*What do you think it is? What do you think it says?*

1_____   6_____   11_____
2_____   7_____   12_____
3_____   8_____   13_____
4_____   9_____   14_____
5_____   10_____   15_____

Note reasoning behind student's response:	*How do you know? What makes you think so?*

1_____   6_____   11_____
2_____   7_____   12_____
3_____   8_____   13_____
4_____   9_____   14_____
5_____   10_____   15_____

Note the part of the graphic display to which student is responding:	*What tells you that it says . . . ? Show me with your finger where it says . . .*

1_____   6_____   11_____
2_____   7_____   12_____
3_____   8_____   13_____
4_____   9_____   14_____
5_____   10_____   15_____

Figure 3–3, p. 34

Child's Concepts of Reading

Name: _____ Date_____ Age_____

1. Do you know how to read?

   If yes:

   a. How did you learn how to read?

   b. Did somebody help you to learn or did you learn by yourself? (If yes, who?)

   c. Do you like to read?

   d. What do you like to read?

   If no:

   a. Do you want to be able to read?

   b. How will you learn to read?

   c. Does someone have to help you learn how to read?

   d. Who do you think will help you learn how to read?

2. Is it possible to learn to read by yourself?

3. Is learning to read easy or hard?

4. Why do you think learning to read is easy/hard?

5. Do the people you live with know how to read?

   a. What do they read?

   b. Where do they read? (kitchen, living room)

   c. What language do they read?

6. Do the people you live with ever read to you?

   a. Who?

   b. What do they read?

   c. In what language do they read to you?

   d. Do you like it? Why?

7. What do you look at while you are being read to? Anything else?

8. a. If I said, "I'm going to read you a story," what would I do?

   b. If I said, "I'm going to tell you a story," what would I do?

   c. Are reading a story and telling a story the same or different? How?

9. Can you read with your eyes closed? How?

10. Do you have a TV? Is there anything to read on TV? Do you have a computer? What is there to read on a computer?

11. Do you ever go to the store?

    a. Is there anything in the store that you read or people can read?

    b. What? (Try to get at books, magazines, newspapers, signs, and labels without using those words. If not, ask directly about them.)

12. Why do people read?

Adapted from Y. Goodman (1992)

Figure 4–1, p. 44

Informal Observation of Book Knowledge

Child's Name: _____

Instructions: Use the blank spaces to fill in the dates on which the following concepts are observed.

Handling

_____ Holds book in an upright position.

_____ Understands that print proceeds from left to right and top to bottom.

_____ Turns pages left to right.

_____ Reads print on left page before right page.

_____ Appropriately uses terms such as *cover*, *page*, *story*, *title*, and *author*. Others:
_____.

_____ Uses book title and cover illustration to make predictions.

_____ Understands that a book contains an author's message.

_____ Understands that an illustrator creates the visuals for a book.

_____ _____

_____ _____

Print Knowledge

_____ Understands that pictures are viewed and print is read.

_____ Knows what a *letter* is (names or points to a letter when asked; uses the term conventionally during conversations).

_____ Knows what a *word* is (names or points to a word when asked; uses the term conventionally during conversations).

_____ Participates in reading when the language is predictable.

_____ Attempts to match voice with print.

_____ Reads some words conventionally.

_____ _____

_____ _____

Interpretive Knowledge

_____ Is eager to select a book to read alone or to someone else.

_____ Is aware that books contain stories as well as other kinds of information.

_____ Labels pictures while looking through the pages of a book.

_____ Uses pictures to make up a connected story or sequence of events.

_____ Discusses/retells stories, referring to ___ character, ___ setting, ___ problem, ___ plot episodes, ___ resolution, ___ theme.

_____ Discusses/retells key concepts and information learned from nonfiction.

_____ Retelling occurs in a logical sequence.

_____ Makes personal connections with books.

_____ Makes connections between books.

_____ _____

_____ _____

Figure 4–2, p. 45

Book-Handling and Print Concepts

Child's Name: _____ Date:_____

Choose a simple storybook. Title: _____

I would like you to read this book for me. Have you seen or read it before? _____ .

If child says NO: If child says YES:
What do you think this book is about?   *What was the book about?*
_____ Uses illustrations   _____ Brief response
_____ Uses illustrations and makes   _____ Detailed response
      additional inferences   _____ Uses print
_____ Uses print

Show me the front of the book. Show me the back. Where is the title?
_____ Front   _____ Back   _____ Title

*Open the book to where the story begins. Response:*_____

Show me where you read. Use your finger to show me how you read.
_____ Points to pictures _____ Points to words
_____ Goes left to right _____ Uses return sweep

Read the book. (If the child refuses, prompt with *Pretend to read* or *Use the pictures*.)
_____ No response
_____ Uses picture cues to label
_____ Uses picture cues to construct a meaningful, connected story
_____ Reads some of the words in the book
_____ Reads the words

After reading, the child:
_____ Can point to a capital letter; _____ lowercase letter.
_____ Can frame one word; _____ two words; _____ first word; _____ last word.
_____ Can frame one letter; _____ two letters; _____ first letter; _____ last letter.
_____ Can frame a period; _____ a comma; _____ a question mark; _____ quotation marks.
_____ Can track 4–5 lines of print as you read them.
_____ Can read some words. List:_____

Tell me something about the story: _____

_____

_____

_____

Did you like this book? _____ *Why?* _____

_____

_____

_____

Figure 4–3, p. 45

Book-Handling Knowledge

Name: _____ Date_____ Age_____

Item	Administration	Instruction	Possible Responses	Child's Response
1	Show book; title covered by hand.	"What's this?" If child answers with name of book, record and ask, "What's (name of book given by child, e.g., *The Hungry Caterpillar*)?"	"book" "storybook" "story" name of book	
2	Display book.	"What do you do with it?"	"read it" "look at it" "tell it" "open it"	
3		"What's inside it?"	"story" "picture" "words" "pages" "letters" "things"	
4	Hold on to a page.	"Show me a page in this book." "Is this a page?"	Points to page. "yes"	
5		"Show me the top of this page." "Show me the bottom of this page."	Indicates top edge or toward top. Indicates bottom of page or toward bottom.	
6	Present book upside down and back toward child.	"Show me the front of this book." "Take the book and open it so that we can read it."	Any indication of front or first page. Opens to first page.	
7		"Show me the beginning of the story." "Show me the end of the story."	Points to first line or word of story. Turns to last page and points to last line or word.	

Figure 4–4, pp. 46–47

(continues)

Book-Handling Knowledge (*continued*)·

Item	Administration	Instruction	Possible Responses	Child's Response
8	Turn back to beginning of story.	"Show me with your finger exactly where we have to begin reading."	Points to first word on page.	
9		"Show me with your finger which way we go as we read this page."	Left to right, on the page, with return sweep.	
10		"Where then?" (This may already have been done or stated in #8 or #9; if so, check off, but do not repeat.)	Top line to bottom line, with return sweep.	
11		"Read the book to me." If child declines, say, "Pretend to read it."	Record all responses.	
12	If child doesn't read book, or after child reads, continue.	"Now I'm going to read you this story. Show me where to start reading. Where do I begin?"	Indicates print on first page.	
13	Read one page.	"You point to the story while I read it." (Read slowly.)	Almost always matches spoken with written words. Sometimes matches spoken with written words.	
14	If there is print on both pages, display the pages. Read to end of story.	"Where do I go now?"	Points to the first line of print on the next page.	
15	If possible, turn to a page with print and a picture on it. Turn book upside down.	"Can you or I read this now?" "Why or why not?"	"Upside down."	

Figure 4–4, pp. 46–47

(continues)

Book-Handling Knowledge (*continued*)

Item	Administration	Instruction	Possible Responses	Child's Response
16	Show student how to use masking cards to close "curtains" over "window." (Use two pieces of dark cardboard.)	"Let's put some of the story in this window. I want you to close the curtains like this until I can see just one letter." "Now just two letters."	One letter correct. Two letters correct.	
17	Open "curtains."	"Now close it until we can see just one word." "Now just two words."	One word correct. Two words correct.	
18	Open "curtains."	"Show me the first letter in a word, any word." "Show me the last letter in a word."	First correct. Last correct.	
19	Remove cards.	"Show me a capital letter, any capital letter."	Points clearly to a capital letter. Points to any letter.	
20	Close book and pass it to child.	"Show me the name of the book (or story)."	Cover, flyleaf, or title page.	
21	Get at comprehension.	"Tell me something about the story."	Record response.	
22	Title page pointing.	"It says here (read title) 'by (read author).' What does 'by (author's name, e.g., Angela Johnson)' mean?"	Responds appropriately.	
23	Title page pointing.	"It says here that the book is illustrated by (read illustrator). What does that mean?"	Responds appropriately.	

Figure 4–4, pp. 46–47

Talk Contexts

_____ Whole Class _____ Individual Child: _____	
Self-Talk	
One-to-One with Adult	
One-to-One with Peers (record peer names)	
Self-Chosen Peer Group (list names)	
Teacher-Chosen Peer Group (needs-based; children who seldom talk in groups; children who talk often; etc.)	
Small Instructional Group (observe across changes in subject matter)	
Whole Group	
Play Settings	

Figure 5–1, p. 55

© 2002 by Gretchen Owocki and Yetta Goodman from _Kidwatching: Documenting Children's Literacy Development_. Portsmouth, NH: Heinemann.

Oral Language Functions: Classroom Observation

Place a check by the functions that are regularly present in your classroom. Place a star by those that occur in various contexts and settings. Indicate the extent to which languages other than English are used to serve the varying functions.

_____ Sharing stories

_____ Retelling events

_____ Reporting information

_____ Explaining how to do or make something

_____ Expressing language and literacy knowledge

_____ Building productive learning relationships with peers and adults

_____ Creating imaginative worlds (during play; through writing or drawing; while singing)

_____ Taking social action

_____ Planning events

_____ Enjoying language for its aesthetic value (poetry; language play)

_____ Describing sensory experiences (sights, smells, sounds, touches, tastes)

_____ Expressing feelings, empathy, emotional identification

_____ Expressing points of view

_____ Taking leadership

_____ Asking questions; requesting information

_____ Building collaborative relations

_____ Responding to peers' and teachers' questions and requests for information

_____ _____

_____ _____

Figure 5–3, p. 57

Oral Language Functions: Individual Observation

Child's Name: _____ Date _____ Age _____

Shares stories

Retells events

Explains how to do or make something

Creates imaginative worlds (during play; through writing or drawing; while singing)

Plans events

Enjoys language for its aesthetic value (poetry; language play)

Expresses feelings, empathy, emotional identification

Takes leadership

Figure 5–4, p. 57

Interactional Competencies

Child's Name: _____

_____ Participates in group talk activities (discussions, poetry reading, dramatization, play, shared writing).

_____ Elaborates coherently on self-selected topics.

_____ Elaborates coherently on instructional topics.

_____ Asks peers questions (for assistance; about language; about content).

_____ Asks teacher questions (for assistance; about language; about content).

_____ Responds appropriately to peer questions, elaborating when relevant.

_____ Responds appropriately to teacher questions, elaborating when relevant.

_____ Participates and takes turns appropriately in conversations.

_____ Leads conversations.

_____ Builds on what others say.

_____ Uses appropriate nonverbal behavior (gestures; facial expressions; ways of indicating listening).

_____ When talking, holds the attention of others.

_____ Speaks clearly and audibly; uses comprehensible speech.

_____ Feels comfortable speaking before a group.

_____ Shows awareness of listener needs (recycles, repairs, clarifies).

_____ Listens when others speak (in one-to-one settings, small groups, large groups).

_____ Uses effective strategies for interrupting.

_____ Demonstrates understanding of oral directions given in a variety of settings.

_____ Talks about language.

_____ Adapts language to changes in setting.

_____ _____

_____ _____

Figure 5–5, p. 58

Miscue Analysis Kidwatching Profile

Reader _____ Age/Grade_____ Date_____

Teacher _____ Selection _____

A. *Comprehending Information*

Does the sentence with or without miscues after the reader has finally read it make sense in the story/article? Mark YES on the typescript next to all sentences without any miscues; sentences with miscues that make sense; and sentences where the unacceptable miscues are self-corrected. Mark NO next to the unacceptable sentences. Then fill in the following information:

1. Number of sentences in the story/article. Total Number: _____
2. Number of sentences marked YES. Total Number: _____
3. Divide total number in 2 by total number in 1 to get percent of sentences in story/article that are semantically acceptable or make sense. _____%

B. *Grammatical or Syntactic Knowledge*

Number of sentences that do not make sense but maintain grammatical structure: _____

List typical examples:_____

_____

_____

_____

_____

C. *Phonics and Graphophonic Knowledge*

1. Total # of word-for-word substitutions: _____   # of High Similarity: _____
   # of Some Similarity: _____
2. Divide # of High/Some by total substitutions.   High Similarity: _____%
   Some Similarity: _____%

List examples:

High Similarity	Some Similarity
_____for_____	_____for_____
_____for_____	_____for_____
_____for_____	_____for_____
_____for_____	_____for_____

List miscues with no similarity and circle Yes or No, depending on whether they result in acceptability within the story/article.

_____for_____ Yes No   _____for_____ Yes No

_____for_____ Yes No   _____for_____ Yes No

_____for_____ Yes No   _____for_____ Yes No

Figure 6–3, p. 76   *(continues)*

Miscue Analysis Kidwatching Profile (*continued*)

D. *Repeated Miscues* (List the same word that is miscued on more than once during the reading.)

Text Word: List each substitution and/or omission and number of each occurrence:

_____   _____

_____   _____

_____   _____

_____   _____

_____   _____

E. *Retelling Information*

The retelling provides evidence of the reader's comprehension of the story/article. Circle the
statement that is most applicable:

Plot/General Idea	Complete	Some	Minimal
Supporting Details/Events	Complete	Some	Minimal

Inferences (Indicate major or minor.):

_____

_____

_____

_____

_____

Misconceptions (Indicate major or minor.):

_____

_____

_____

_____

_____

Figure 6–3, p. 76

Kidwatching Profile Summary

List statistics and relevant comments.

Semantic Acceptability (the degree to which the reader is comprehending or making sense)

Yes_____% No _____%

Examples for discussion purposes:

_____

_____

Syntactic Acceptability (the degree to which the reading sounds like language)

Examples for discussion purposes:

_____

_____

Graphophonic Similarity (the degree to which the reader is using phonics and graphophonic knowledge)

High_____% Some _____%

Examples for discussion purposes:

_____

_____

Meaning Change (Examples of miscues that change the meaning.): _____

_____

Retelling (Use child's language to document comprehension.) Holistic Score _____

_____

_____

_____

_____

Comments about the reader and the reading:_____

_____

Plans for strategy lessons and other reading instruction: _____

_____

Figure 6–4, p. 76

© 2002 by Gretchen Owocki and Yetta Goodman from *Kidwatching: Documenting Children's Literacy Development*. Portsmouth, NH: Heinemann.

Written Language Functions, Formats, and Genres

_____Advertisements

_____Alphabet books

_____Announcements (birth, death)

_____Autobiographies

_____Bills

_____Biographies

_____Blueprints

_____Book jackets

_____Calendars

_____Cartoons and comics

_____Charts and graphs

_____Checks

_____Computer software/publishing programs

_____Coupons

_____Diagrams

_____Expressions of opinion

_____Forms

_____Health records

_____Instant messaging

_____Instructions (for games, crafts)

_____Internet search engines

_____Invitations

_____Journals and logs

_____Labels

_____Letters, email, notes, and cards

_____Lists

_____Maps

_____Menus

_____Observational notes

_____Nonfiction in varied genres

_____Pamphlets

_____Phone messages

_____Plans for events

_____Poems and songs

_____Posters

_____Price tags

_____Programs (for theater, events)

_____Receipts

_____Recipes

_____Records of events

_____Reports (weather, sports, scientific)

_____Requests for information

_____Restaurant orders

_____Reviews (of books, movies, TV shows)

_____Rules

_____Schedules

_____Scripts

_____Self-evaluations and reflections

_____Signs

_____Stories (in varied genres)

_____Tickets

_____Webs

_____Word puzzles and games

_____ _____

_____ _____

_____ _____

_____ _____

Figure 7–2, p. 80

Concepts of Written and Pictorial Representation

Name: _____ Date_____ Grade_____

Procedures: Offer a variety of paper and writing utensils. The italicized phrases are suggestions to use to engage the child in writing. Ask the child to respond to each item, document all verbal and nonverbal responses, and save the child's drawing and writing (or a copy), recording the date, the context, and any other pertinent information.

1. Offer the materials and encourage the child to *Write something.* If the child declines, suggest that he or she *Pretend to write.*

2. *Read me what you wrote.* If child says, "I can't," ask why, and then suggest that the child *Pretend to read.*

3. *Tell me about what you wrote. What are this and this?* (Get at the terms *word, letter, sentence, period, question mark,* and so on.)

4. *Write a letter.* (Children may respond with an alphabetic letter or write a letter to someone.)

5. *What do you write at home?*

6. *What do you write at school?*

7. *Why do people write? What kinds of things do they write? Can you write (or pretend to write) any of these things?*

8. *Draw a picture.*

Figure 7–6, p. 83   *(continues)*

9. Make sure the child is looking directly at his/her writing and drawing.

   a. *Show me your writing. Show me your drawing.*

   b. *Is drawing the same as writing?*

   c. *How are they alike (the same; like each other)? How are they different?*

10. Enlarge the following samples to fit on a single sheet of paper or cut each apart to fit on separate cards. Ask the child *Which of these are writing? Why do you think so?*

bread	n'est-ce pas?	⇨	T5A28B
go	✈	ᴧᴧ ᴧᴧ ᴧᴧ ᴧᴧ ᴧᴧ ᴧᴧ	K
FFFFFF	*kitten*	📫	piñata
●❖⊠⌘	Get on the bike.	**RESTROOMS**	▼△◄▷ ◣◥

11. Invite the child to write his/her name. *Do you know how to write any other names?*

12. Write three different-looking names including the child's and ask him/her to point to his/her name and read it.

Adapted from Y. Goodman (1992)

Figure 7–6, p. 83

Spelling Knowledge

Child's Name: _____ Date _____

_____ Represents meaning using random strings of letters

_____ Uses prominent sounds to spell words (often, these are consonants in English; vowels in Spanish)

_____ Uses one letter to represent each word or syllable (S for *star*; BT for *better*)

_____ Uses initial and final consonants to represent syllables or words (SR for *star*; BDR for *better*)

_____ Incorporates medial consonant and vowel letters (STAR; BEDR)

_____ Spells short vowels conventionally

_____ Uses vowel markers (more than one vowel) to spell long vowels conventionally

_____ Uses phonics to spell past-tense endings (WAKT for *walked*; ADID for *added*; SNOWD for *snowed*)

_____ Uses visual features (-ed) to spell past-tense endings conventionally

_____ Uses double consonants consistently (*better*; *ladder*)

_____ Demonstrates knowledge of spelling patterns such as -ing, -ate, -ain, -er, and -es

_____ Continues to increase visual memory/repertoire of words usually spelled conventionally

_____ Recognizes when words are misspelled

_____ Continues to invent spellings for low-frequency words (words not frequently used in the child's writing)

Figure 7–7, p. 85

Note-Taking Form for Observing Writing

Child's Name: _____ Date _____

What to Look For	Examples and Instances
Knowledge about the functions of writing (e.g., uses writing for varied purposes; writes on varied topics; explores functions in play; knows when to use a list, web, envelope, note, card, sign)	
Knowledge about written language formats and genres (e.g., writes in varied genres; uses different forms; uses typical generic features; invents new features)	
Knowledge about ideas and content that are expressed in writing (e.g., content is connected to personal life and classroom inquiries; content fits the format and genre; humor and sensitivity develop in appropriate genres)	
Knowledge about orthography and phonology (e.g., forms letters; understands that print means; knows difference between drawing and writing; represents written language syllabically; shows alphabetic knowledge)	
Knowledge about punctuation (e.g., explores use of spacing, line breaks, periods, commas, question marks, capitalization, dialogue markers, font variations)	
Knowledge of grammar (e.g., sentences are complete in narrative; words or phrases are used appropriately in specific genres; dialogue is used)	
Processes of getting ideas on paper (e.g., solves problems collaboratively; asks for help; invents spellings; copies items around the room; uses pictionary or dictionary; uses private speech; uses talk, drawing, movement, and sound)	
Social processes (e.g., works collaboratively with others; talks about writing; sensitively and thoughtfully responds to others' ideas; conferences; participates in author's chair)	
View of self as writer/author	

Figure 7–8, p. 88

Profile of Writing Knowledge

Child's Name: _____ Grade_____

Knowledge Demonstrated:	Sept	Nov	Jan	Mar	May	Description/Examples/ Reflections
Draws to signify meaning						
Uses invented characters to signify meaning						
Shows a sense of directionality						
Uses random strings of letters to signify meaning						
Writes letters to represent beginning or prominent sounds						
Writes letters to represent vowels and medial consonants						
Is beginning to conventionally spell commonly used words						
Uses spacing between words						
Uses capitalization for names and places						
Writes sentences with appropriate grammatical form						
Uses simple punctuation (.?!); more complex punctuation (",')						
Chooses own topics for drawing and writing						
Writes with sensitivity						
Explores varying voices (serious, informative, humorous)						
Shares pictures and writing with others						
Rereads own writing/revises/ edits						
Explores multiple genres						
Self-evaluates						

Figure 7–9, p. 90

Peer Conference Form

Writer: _____

Reader: _____

What the writer likes:

What the reader likes:

The writer will work on:

Figure 7–12, p. 92

Bibliography

Adelman, C. 1992. "Play as a Quest for Vocation." *Journal of Curriculum Studies* 24(2): 139–51.

Barnes, D. 1993. "Supporting Exploratory Talk for Learning." In *Cycles of Meaning*, edited by K. Pierce and C. Gilles, 17–34. Portsmouth, NH: Heinemann.

Barr, M., D. Craig, D. Fysette, and M. Syverson. 1999. *Assessing Literacy with the Learning Record*. Portsmouth, NH: Heinemann.

Bredekamp, S., and C. Copple. 1997. *Developmentally Appropriate Practice in Early Childhood Programs*. Washington, DC: National Association for the Education of Young Children.

Brown, J., K. Goodman, and A. Marek. 1996. *Studies in Miscue Analysis: An Annotated Bibliography*. Newark, DE: International Reading Association.

Bruner, J. 1983. "Play, Thought, and Language." *Peabody Journal of Education* 60: 60–69.

Carle, E. 1969. *The Very Hungry Caterpillar*. New York: Philomel.

Clay, M. 1972. *The Sand Test*. Portsmouth, NH: Heinemann.

Cowley, J. 1999. *Mrs. Wishy-Washy*. New York: Philomel.

Dewey, J. [1910] 1997. *How We Think*. Toronto, ON: Dover.

Doake, D. 1988. *Book Experience and Emergent Reading in Preschool Children*. Vols. 1 and 2. Unpublished doctoral dissertation, Department of Elementary Education, University of Alberta, Edmonton, AB.

Duckett, P. 2001. First-Grade Beginning Readers' Use of Pictures and Print as They Read. Unpublished doctoral dissertation, University of Arizona, Tucson, AZ.

Dyson, A. 1989. *Multiple Worlds of Child Writers*. New York: Teachers College Press.

———. 2001. "Where Are the Childhoods in Childhood Literacy? An Exploration in Outer (School) Space." *Journal of Early Childhood Literacy* 1(1): 9–39.

Dyson, A., and S. Freedman. 1991 "On Teaching Writing: A Review of the Literature." In *Handbook of Research on Teaching the English Language Arts*, edited by J. Squire, J. Jensen, J. Flood, and D. Lapp, 754–74. New York: Macmillan.

Erickson, F. 1986. "Qualitative Methods in Research on Teaching." In *Handbook of Research on Teaching*, edited by E. Wittrock, 119–61. New York: Macmillan.

Faltis, C. 1997. *Joinfostering: Adapting Teaching for the Multilingual Classroom*. Upper Saddle River, NJ: Merrill.

Ferreiro, E. 1990. "Literacy Development: Psychogenesis." In *How Children Construct Literacy*, edited by Y. Goodman, 26–44. Newark, DE: International Reading Association.

Ferreiro, E., and A. Teberosky. 1982. *Literacy Before Schooling*. Trans. K. Castro. Portsmouth, NH: Heinemann.

Flurkey, A. 1997. "Inventing Learning Disabilities." In *Teaching and Advocacy*, edited by D. Taylor, 211–38. York, ME: Stenhouse.

Gee, J. 1999. "Critical Issues: Reading and the New Literacy Studies: Reframing the National Academy of Sciences Report on Reading." In *Journal of Literacy Research* 31(3): 355–74.

———. 2000. "Discourse and Sociocultural Studies in Reading." In *Handbook of Reading Research*, Volume III, edited by M. Kamil, P. Mosenthal, P. D. Pearson, and R. Barr, 195–207. Mahwah, NJ: Erlbaum.

Goodman, K. 1986. *What's Whole in Whole Language?* Portsmouth, NH: Heinemann.

———. 1991. "Evaluation in Whole Language." In *The Whole Language Catalog*, edited by K. Goodman, L. Bridges Bird, and Y. Goodman, 252. Santa Rosa, CA: American School Publishers.

———. 1996a. *On Reading*. Portsmouth, NH: Heinemann.

———. 1996b. "Principles of Revaluing." In *Retrospective Miscue Analysis: Revaluing Readers and Reading*, edited by Y. Goodman and A. Marek, 13–20. Katonah, NY: Richard C. Owen.

Goodman, K., L. Bridges Bird, and Y. Goodman. 1991. *The Whole Language Catalog*. Santa Rosa, CA: American School Publishers.

Goodman, K., and Y. Goodman. 1990. "Vygotsky in a Whole Language Perspective." In *Vygotsky and Education*, edited by L. Moll, 223–50. Cambridge, MA: Cambridge University Press.

Goodman, Y. 1980. "The Roots of Literacy." In *Claremont Reading Conference 44th Yearbook*, edited by M. Douglass, 1–32. Claremont, CA: Claremont Reading Conference.

———. 1992. "Classroom Demonstrations." In *The Whole Language Catalog: Supplement on Authentic Assessment*, edited by K. Goodman, L. Bridges Bird, and Y. Goodman, 141. Santa Rosa, CA: American Book Publishers.

———. 1996a. *Notes from a Kidwatcher*. Portsmouth, NH: Heinemann.

———. 1996b. "Revaluing Readers While Readers Revalue Themselves: Retrospective Miscue Analysis." *The Reading Teacher* 49(8): 600–609.

———. 1998. *I Had a Little Overcoat*. New York: Mondo.

Goodman, Y., B. Altwerger, and A. Marek. 1989. *Print Awareness in Preschool Children: The Development of Literacy in Preschool Children*. Occasional Paper: Program in Language and Literacy. University of Arizona, Tucson, AZ.

Goodman, Y., and A. Marek. 1996. *Retrospective Miscue Analysis: Revaluing Readers and Reading*. Katonah, NY: Richard C. Owen.

Goodman, Y., D. Watson, and C. Burke. 1987. *Reading Miscue Inventory: Alternative Procedures*. New York: Richard C. Owen.

Graves, D. 1983. *Writing: Teachers and Children at Work*. Portsmouth, NH: Heinemann.

———. 1989. *Exploring Nonfiction*. Portsmouth, NH: Heinemann.

Gundlach, R. 1982. "Children as Writers: The Beginnings of Learning to Write." In *What Writers Know: The Language, Process, and Structure of Written Discourse*, edited by M. Nystrand, 129–48. New York: Academic.

Halliday, M. 1975. *Learning How to Mean: Explorations in the Development of Language*. London: Edward Arnold.

Hawes, J. 1987. *Why Frogs Are Wet*. New York: HarperCollins.

Heath, S. B. 1983. *Ways with Words: Language, Life, and Work in Communities and Classrooms*. Cambridge, England: Cambridge University Press.

Hills, T. 1999. "Critical Issue: Assessing Young Children's Progress Appropriately." North Central Regional Educational Laboratory. *www.ncrel.org*.

Hood, W. 1992. "That Story Makes Sense Now!" In *The Whole Language Catalog: Supplement on Authentic Assessment*, edited by K. Goodman, L. Bridges Bird, and Y. Goodman, 57. Santa Rosa, CA: American Book Publishers.

Howard, C. 1994. "Getting to Know Your Child." In *The Whole Language Catalog: Forms for Authentic Assessment*, edited by L. Bridges Bird, K. Goodman, and Y. Goodman, 129. Boston: McGraw-Hill.

Katz, L., and S. Chard. 1996. "The Contribution of Documentation to the Quality of Early Childhood Education." ERIC/EECE Clearinghouse on Elementary and Early Childhood Education (ED 393608). *http://ericps.crc.vivc.edu/eece/pubs/digests/1996/lkchar96.html*

Language Arts Committee, Palo Alto Unified School District. 1994. "My Child as a Language Learner: Parent Observation Pre-K–1." In *The Whole Language Catalog: Forms for Authentic Assessment*, edited by L. Bridges Bird, K. Goodman, and Y. Goodman, 232. Boston: McGraw-Hill.

Lindfors, J. 1991. *Children's Language and Learning*. Needham Heights, MA: Allyn & Bacon.

Lobel, A. 1979. *Days with Frog and Toad*. New York: Scholastic.

Martens, P. 1997. *I Already Know How to Read: A Child's View of Literacy*. Portsmouth, NH: Heinemann.

McWhorter, J. 2000. *Spreading the Word: Language and Dialect in America*. Portsmouth, NH: Heinemann.

Meek, M. 1997. *How Texts Teach What Readers Learn*. London: Thimble.

Meisels, S. 1995. "Performance Assessment in Early Childhood Education: The Work Sampling System." *ERIC Digest* [Online]. *www.ed.gov/databases/ERIC_Digests/ed382407.html*.

Meyer, R. 1992. "Miscues or Mistakes: Two Teachers and Two Students." In *The Whole Language Catalog: Supplement on Authentic Assessment*, edited by K. Goodman, L. Bridges Bird, and Y. Goodman, 60. Santa Rosa, CA: American Book Publishers.

Mickleson, N. 1990. "Evaluation in Whole Language." In *Readings on Assessing Language Arts*, 1–30. Ontario, Canada: Ministry of Education.

Moll, L., and J. Greenberg. 1990. "Creating Zones of Possibilities: Combining Social Contexts for Instruction." In *Vygotsky and Education*, edited by L. Moll, 319–48. Cambridge, England: Cambridge University Press.

Mooney, M. 1988. *Developing Lifelong Readers*. Katonah, NY: Richard C. Owen.

———. 1990. *Reading to, with, and by Children*. Katonah, NY: Richard C. Owen.

Murphy, S., and C. Dudley-Marling. 2000. "Editors' Pages." *Language Arts* 77(5): 380–81.

Neill, M. 2000. "Transforming Student Assessment." In *Issues and Trends in Literacy Education*, 2d ed., edited by R. Robinson, M. McKenna, and J. Wedman, 136–52. Boston: Allyn & Bacon.

Oakes, J., and M. Lipton. 1999. *Teaching to Change the World*. Boston: McGraw-Hill.

O'Keefe, T. 1996. "Teachers as Kidwatchers." In *Creating Classrooms for Authors and Inquirers*, edited by K. Short and J. Harste with C. Burke, 63–79. Portsmouth, NH: Heinemann.

Owocki, G. 1999. *Literacy Through Play*. Portsmouth, NH: Heinemann.

———. 2001. *Make Way for Literacy!* Portsmouth, NH: Heinemann.

Paley, V. G. 1997. *The Girl with the Brown Crayon*. Cambridge, MA: Harvard University Press.

Phillips, S. 1983. *The Invisible Culture: Communication in Classroom and Community on the Warm Springs Indian Reservation*. Prospect Heights, IL: Waveland.

Piaget, J. 1952. *The Construction of Reality in the Child*. New York: Basic.

Read, C. 1975. *Children's Categorization of Speech Sounds in English*. Urbana, IL: National Council of Teachers of English.

Ruiz, R. 1991. "The Empowerment of Language Minority Students." In *Empowerment Through Multicultural Education*, edited by C. Sleeter, 217–27. Albany, NY: State University of New York.

Salinger, T. 1998. "How Do We Assess Young Children's Literacy Learning?" In *Children Achieving*, edited by S. Neuman and K. Roskos, 223–49. Newark, DE: International Reading Association.

Schickedanz, J. 1999. *Much More Than the ABCs*. Washington, DC: National Association for the Education of Young Children.

Short, K., J. Harste, and C. Burke. 1996. *Creating Classrooms for Authors and Inquirers*. Portsmouth, NH: Heinemann.

Smitherman, G. 1999. *Talkin That Talk: African American Language and Culture*. New York: Routledge.

Sowers, S. 1985. "Learning to Write in a Workshop: A Study in Grades One Through Four." In *Advances in Writing Research, Volume One: Children's Early Writing Development*, edited by M. Farr, 297–342. Norwood, NJ: Ablex.

Taylor, D. 1983. *Family Literacy*. Portsmouth, NH: Heinemann.

———. 1988. *Growing Up Literate*. Portsmouth, NH: Heinemann.

———. 1997. *Many Families, Many Literacies: An International Declaration of Principles*. Portsmouth, NH: Heinemann.

Toohey, K. 2000. *Learning English in School: Identity, Social Relations, and Classroom Practice*. Clevedon, England: Multilingual Matters.

Uttech, M. 1997. "*Vale La Pena*: Advocacy Along the Borderlands." In *Teaching and Advocacy*, edited by D. Taylor, D. Coughlin, and J. Marasco, 160–78. York, ME: Stenhouse.

Vygotsky, L. S. 1978. *Mind in Society: The Development of Higher Psychological Processes*, edited and translated by M. Cole, V. John-Steiner, S. Scribner, and E. Souberman. Cambridge, MA: Harvard University Press.

Wells, G. 1990. "Talk: A Medium for Learning and Change: An Inquiry Orientation." In *Readings on Assessing Language Arts*, 77–81. Ontario, Canada: Ministry of Education.

Whitemore, K., and C. Crowell. 1994. "Inventing a Classroom: Life in a Bilingual Whole Language Learning Community." York, ME: Stenhouse.

Whitmore, K., and Y. Goodman. 1995. "Transforming Curriculum in Language and Literacy." In *Reaching Potentials: Transforming Early Childhood Curriculum and Assessment*, Vol. 2, edited by S. Bredekamp and T. Rosegrant, 145–66. Washington, DC: National Association for the Education of Young Children.

Wilde, S. 1992. *You Kan Red This!* Portsmouth, NH: Heinemann.

———. 2000. *Miscue Analysis Made Easy: Building on Student Strengths.* Portsmouth, NH: Heinemann.

Wolfram, W., C. Adger, and D. Christian. 1998. *Dialects in Schools and Communities.* Mahwah, NJ: Erlbaum.

Wood, A. 1992. *Silly Sally.* New York: Harcourt Brace.

Index

Alphabetic hypothesis, 84
Alphabetic principle, 30, 84
Analysis
    data, analyzing, 11–13
    materials for, organizing, 11–12
    miscue (*see* Miscue analysis)
    questions as basis for, 12–13
    of sociocultural aspects of children's literacies,
        23–25
Anecdotal records, 8, 9, 10, 96
    in book-handling observation, 44–45
Assessment. *See* Evaluation

Bible, 16
Book handling, 38–47
    development, 38–43
    evaluation, 45–47, 104–108
    expanding repertoires, 47
    functions of books, 38
    interaction and observation, 43–47
    routines, book sharing, 38–39
Book-handling knowledge task (forms), 45–47,
        104–108
Books. *See also* Written language
    book handling (*see* Book handling)
    directionality and, 40–41
    discourses surrounding, 39–40
    early experiences with, 37–38
    functions of, young children discovering, 38
    holistic remembering, 42–43
    literary forms, developing knowledge of, 41–42
    significance, determining, 41
    text, constructing a meaningful, 40
Bush, Christian, 8–10, 11, 15–19, 53–54

Checklists, 10–11
    book-handling knowledge, documenting, 45–47,
        104–108
    families in the classroom (form), 23, 101
    informal observation of book knowledge (form),
        45, 104
    interactional competencies, 58, 112

my child as language learner (forms), 18, 19, 99,
        100
    oral language functions, classroom observation
        (form), 57, 110
    profile of writing knowledge demonstrated
        (form), 90, 121
    spelling knowledge (form), 85, 119
    written language functions, formats, and genres
        (form), 80, 116
Children, self-evaluation. *See* Self-evaluation,
        student's
Choice, learning and, 22
Clay, Marie, 46
Cognitive tension, 4
Community
    of practice, 22–23
    safe, 54
Concepts, jointly negotiating, 51–52
Conferences, 13–14, 90–92
    parents and, 13
    peer conference form, 92, 122
Contexts, talk, 55, 109
Cumulative records
    in miscue analysis, 72
    in writing development, 92

Data, analyzing, 11–12
Days with Frog and Toad, 64–65
Dewey, John, 3
Directionality, print awareness, 29
Disequilibrium, 4
Displays, evaluating print awareness with print, 32
Doake, David, 46
Documentation. *See also* Evaluation
    anecdotal records and, 8, 9, 10, 96
    of book-handling knowledge, 43–45, 103–105
    checklists and, 10–11
    in data analysis, 12
    field notes and, 8–10, 11
    miscue analysis and, 67–72, 74–76, 113–15
    miscue analysis kidwatching profile (form), 76,
        113–14

Documentation (*continued*)
   miscue analysis kidwatching profile summary
      (form), 76, 115
   observing and documenting children's
      knowledge, 7–11, 96
   of orthographic knowledge, 83–84, 85
   of print awareness, 31–33, 36
   of talk, 55–59, 109–12
   value of, 6
Drawing, and multiple symbol systems, 86–87

Emic view, 3
Environment
   rich (*see* Rich environment)
   that recognizes difference, 59
Environmental print, 31–32, 78–79
Errors, 4. *See also* Miscue analysis; Miscues
Ethnographic perspective, 3
Evaluation
   of book-handling knowledge, 45–47, 104–108
   children's, self-evaluation (*see* Self-evaluation,
      student's)
   documentation (*see* Documentation)
   miscue analysis (*see* Miscue analysis)
   observation (*see* Observation)
   of oral language learning, 55–60, 109–12
   of orthographic knowledge, 83–84, 85
   of print awareness, 31–36, 102
   social-contextual approach to, 17–18, 19, 20,
      97–100
   teacher's, self-evaluation, 14
   using evaluation, to inform instruction, 14
   of writing, 88–92, 120–22
Experience, sociocultural knowledge and. *See*
      Sociocultural knowledge and experience

Families, in rich environments for learning, 22–23
Families in the classroom (form), 23, 101
Fiction, developing awareness of, 41
Field notes, 8–10, 11
Finding out what kids think (forms), 18, 20, 101
Formats, written language, 79–80, 116
Forms, language, 55–56
Functions, language, 55–56

Genres, written language, 79–80, 116
Goodman, Kenneth, 62
Graphophonics, 80–81

High-quality miscues, 63
Holistic remembering, 42–43

Identity
   language and, 18–20
   as a writer, developing, 87–88
I Had a Little Overcoat, 65
Informational print, 79
Insertions, miscues, 68

Insider view, building an, 3
Interaction
   with children, 6–7
   interactional competencies, observing, 57–58,
      112
Interactional competencies (form), 58, 112
Interests, 54
Interpretive probing, 6–7
Inventions in language learning, role of, 7–8

Kidwatching
   basic acts of, 2–3
   children's self-evaluation, fostering, 13–14
   components, 3–14
   data, analyzing, 11–13
   defined, 1–14
   insider view in, 3
   interacting with children, 6
   language and literacy development in, 3–6
   rich environment, organizing a, 6
   self-evaluation of teaching, 14
   using evaluation to inform instruction, 14
Knowledge
   construction, 3–4
   demonstrated through talk, observing, 58–59
   funds of knowledge, 22–23
   observing and documenting children's, 7–11, 96
   oral language as medium for jointly constructing,
      50–51
   sociocultural experience and (*See* Sociocultural
      knowledge and experience)
Koran, 16

Language
   development, understanding language, 3–6
   differences, 59
   enculturation, 16–17
   functions and forms, observing, 55–57, 110–11
   and identity, 18–20
   knowledge construction, 3–4
   personal and sociocultural influences, 4–6
   reasons to use, 54
   as sociocultural practice, 16–20
Learning
   knowledge construction, 3–4
   personal and sociocultural influences, 4–6
Length, in print awareness, 28–29
Literacy
   development, understanding literacy, 3–6
   enculturation, 16–17
   knowledge construction, 3–4
   personal and sociocultural influences, 4–6
   politics and, 25–26

Miscue analysis, 63–76
   cumulative records, keeping, 72
   documenting and analyzing miscues, 67–72,
      74–76, 113–15

extra support, miscue analysis for children needing, 65–66
formal, 68–69, 113–15
forms, 76, 113–14, 115
for individual and group instruction, 64–65
informal, 70–71
material gathering for, 72–73
proficient readers, miscue analysis for, 65–66
purpose of, 63, 67
rationale and background, 62–63
retellings, 71–72
for whole-class discussion, 65
Miscue analysis kidwatching profile (form), 76, 113–14
Miscue analysis kidwatching profile summary (form), 76, 115
Miscues
defined, 62–63
documenting, 67–72, 74–76, 113–15
high-quality, 63
in language learning, role of, 7–8, 63
oral reading and (see Miscue analysis; Miscues)
sociocultural basis for, 4
Mooney, Margaret, 72
Mrs. Wishy-Washy, 37
Multiple symbol systems, use of, 86–87

New Baby Calf, The, 61
Nonfiction, developing awareness of, 41

Observation. See also Evaluation
anecdotal records and, 8, 9, 10, 96
of book-handling knowledge, 43–45, 103–105
central task of, 8
checklists and, 10–11
field notes and, 8–10, 11
informal observation of book knowledge (form), 45, 104
note-taking form for observations, 9–10, 96
observing and documenting children's knowledge, 7–11, 96
of print awareness, 31–33, 35–36
of talk, 55–59, 109–12
of writing, 88, 120
Occupational print, 79
Omissions, miscues, 68
Open-ended prompts, 89
Oral language, 48–60
books, oral discourses surrounding, 39–40
contexts, talk, 55, 109
evaluation, 55–60, 109–12
in human development, 49–50
interactions with children, 51–53
jointly negotiating concepts with, 51–52
letting child do the talking, 51
materials for analysis, collecting, 12
in multiple symbol systems, 86

oral reading and miscues (see Miscue analysis; Miscues)
reflection, encouraging, 52
responses, providing substantive, 52–53
rich talk environment, providing a, 53–55
student self-evaluation of, 59–60
symbols relate to sounds, understanding how, 30–31
thinking and learning, as medium for, 49–50
value of, 49–51
and written language, correspondence between, 29–30
Oral reading and miscues. See Miscue analysis; Miscues
Orthography
assessment, 83–84, 117–18
defined, 78, 80
knowledge, orthographic, 81–83, 85–86
punctuation, 85–86
Ownership, learning and, 22

Paraphrasing, 35
Parents
conferences and, 13
evaluating child's language learning, 17–18, 19, 20, 97–100
observation forms, 18, 19, 98, 99
Peer conference form, 92, 122
Personal influences, 4–6
Phonology
defined, 78, 80
knowledge, phonological, 84–85
Photo shoots, evaluating print awareness with, 32
Piaget, Jean, 4
Play, evaluating print awareness during, 32–33
Politics, literacy and, 25–26
Portfolio, 12
Print awareness, 27–36
assessment data, 36
developmental moments, 28–31
directionality, 29
evaluating, 31–36, 102
evaluating, forms for, 34, 102
expanding competencies, 36
oral language and writing, correspondence between, 29–30
size and length, 28–29
symbols and, 28, 30–31
unique designs, 29
word, concept of, 29
Prompts, 89
Punctuation, 85–86

Questions
analyzing print awareness with, 34–36, 102
as basis for analysis, 12–13
child's concepts of reading (form), 44, 103
for evaluating talk, 56

Questions (*continued*)
 finding out what kids think (form), 18, 20, 101
 getting to know your child (form), 17–18, 97–98
 for student self-evaluation, 60

Reading
 analyzing, collecting materials for, 12
 child's concepts of (form), 44, 103
 directionality and, 40–41
 literary forms and, 42
 miscues (*see* Miscue analysis; Miscues)
 print awareness (*see* Print awareness)
 print to meaning, development of, 43
Reading Miscue Inventory, 67
Recreational print, 79
Reflection, encouraging, 52
Reggio Emilia approach to education, 6
Register, 42
Relevance, learning and, 22
Rephrasing, 35
Reproducibles, 95–122
Retellings, miscue analysis and, 71, 72
Rich environment
 defined, 5–6
 families involved with, 22–23
 organizing a, 6
 relevance, ownership, and choice in a, 22
 sociocultural perspective in, 21–23
Routines, book sharing, 38–39

Safe community, 54
Scrapbooks, evaluating print awareness with, 32
Segmentation, 85
Self-evaluation, student's
 fostering, 13–14
 of oral language, 59–60
 of writing, 90–92, 122
Self-evaluation, teacher's, 14
Self-reflection, teacher's
 engaging in, 2
 sociocultural perspectives and, 24–25
Semantic acceptability, 69
Size, in print awareness, 28–29
Socialization, promoting, 54
Sociocultural knowledge and experience, 15–26
 assessing, aspects of children's literacy, 23–25
 community of practice, building a, 26
 evaluation practices, 17–18, 19, 20, 97–100
 family language practices, varied, 16–17
 identity, language and, 18–20
 influences, 4–6
 language as sociocultural practice, 16–20, 78–79
 perspective, on language and literacy, 3, 4–6
 rich environment for learning, organizing a (*see* Rich environment)
 transcending politics, 25–26
 written language, sociocultural factors in, 78–79
Sociolinguistic theory, 16

Speech. *See* Oral language
Spelling knowledge, 84–85, 119
Substantive responses, providing, 52–53
Substitutions, miscues, 68
Syllabic hypothesis, 84
Symbols, in print awareness. *See* Print awareness
Syntactic acceptability, 69–70

Talk. *See* Oral language
Talk contexts, 55, 109
Teachers
 prompts, teacher-directed, 89
 self-evaluation (*see* Self-evaluation, teacher's)
 self-reflection, 2
Teaching, effective, 3
Think-aloud, 1–2

Under One Sun Desert School (Arizona), 39

Very Hungry Caterpillar, The, 40
Vygotsky, Lev, 6, 49–50

Whitmore, Jacquie, 1–3
Why Frogs Are Wet, 66
Wilde, Sandra, 67
Word, concept of, 29
Word study centers, evaluating print awareness
 with, 32
Writing, 77–93
 analyzing, collecting materials for, 12
 cumulative records, 92
 evaluating, 88–92, 120–22
 identity as a writer, developing, 87–88
 multiple symbol systems, use of, 86–87
 open-ended prompts, 89
 oral language and, correspondence between, 29–30
 print awareness (*see* Print awareness)
 punctuation, 85–86
 samples, collecting, 88–89
 self-evaluation, student, 90–92, 122
 teacher-directed prompts, 89
Written and pictorial representation assessment, 83–84, 117–18
Written language. *See also* Books
 directionality, 40–41
 formats, 79–80, 116
 functions, 78–79
 genres, 79–80, 116
 graphophonics and, 80–81, 83–84
 orthography (*see* Orthography)
 phonology (*See* Phonology)
 print to meaning, development of, 43
 registers, knowledge of written language, 42
Written text
 literary forms, developing knowledge of, 41–42
 significance, determining, 41

Zone of proximal development, 6, 50